Nectar of Nondual Truth

CONTENTS

10 Survival of the Fittest
by Swami Sunirmalananda
Placing a unique twist on this oft-repeated phrase, this convincing article reveals the real meaning of words such as "strength" and "fitness," aligning them with words like "compassion" and "love." The principle of true Existence is thus rendered clear and desirable.

12 Vivekananda & His Women Disciples
by Professor Sharad Chandra
In the impressive sweep that heralded Swami Vivekananda's timely appearance in the West, it was the presence of a group of highly qualified women that mainly paved the way to his overall success here.

15 Early Christian Asceticism
by Professor Edward T. Ulrich
Renunciation, though foreign to the public sector in general, and to conventional religion, is nevertheless the very essence of authentic religion. This is true not only of those religions whose especial earmarks are detachment and transcendence, but also of those traditions whose pathways have been cut in the very foundation of the world.

18 Pilgrimage to Pavapuri
by Swami Brahmeshananda
In this installment on Jainism, the reader is ushered into the sacred precincts of the holy Jain temple compound and its devotional way of life. As the swami states in his inspiring article, *"...the shrine has an unusual serenity, and the mind becomes calm and indrawn as soon as one enters it. Here one need not, rather, must not, try to control the mind, but must relax and allow the peace and holiness of the place to permeate one's being."*

27 The Wonder of Universality
by Babaji Bob Kindler
There are stages to a culture's maturation over time, and to humanity's spiritual refinement. The best barometer for these types of progress is the principle of Universality, wherein the very best of mankind's aspiration is combined with actual practice in the open-minded atmosphere of support for all World Religions.

32 Taking Hand in Sufism
by Sheikh Nur al-Jerrahi
With its Four Levels and Seven Steps, the blessing of "taking hand" in Sufism is described in detail, utilizing precious imagery and direct personal experience.

37 Prayer and the Knowledge of G-d
by Rabbi Eli Mallon
The superlative Jewish song, Adan Olam, is taken up for consideration in this stirring testament to its powers of transformation.

40 Inlakech — You Are My Other Me
by David Escobar
Nectar journal is delighted to present its first article representing one of the sacred indigenous religions of the world, whose ties to mother earth and her living spirit still run deep and strong.

42 Song from the Heart
by Dzogchen Ponlop Rinpoche
The immeasurably great blessing of the Lineage Gurus is the subject of this article, woven with subtle wisdom threads into the foundational fabric of the Dakpo Kagyu tradition of Tibetan Buddhism.

49 Spiritual Discernment
by Paravasta Sam Bailey
An in-depth examination of the principle of spiritual discrimination forms the content of this expose, set in the context of several world traditions.

55 Advaitic Judaism
by Rabbi Rami Shapiro
In another offering of the rabbi's sharing of wisdom in the Jewish tradition, he cites ample proof and support for the presence of Nonduality in and throughout the Jewish scriptures and its teachings.

57 On Swami Vivekananda
by Swami Aseshananda
In an ongoing testament to this late, great swami, Nectar of Nondual Truth is pleased to offer a transcription of another of his glowing discourses.

> "There should be no place where the halcyon Light of Advaita Vedanta should not reach or go. This is the decree of Swami Vivekananda, the harbinger of uncompromised Nonduality in this day and age ..."

Publisher's Page

Sarada Ramakrishna Vivekananda – SRV Associations
"Setting the feet of humanity on the path of Universal Truth."

Notes on an Advaitic Journal

At the basis of Advaita as the philosophy of Shankara and his gurus, there is Advaita as experience. Advaita as experience represents that supreme place where all diversity merges in its Essence. It is not combatant or immiscible with qualified or dualistic approaches, but rather provides them their place of consummate arrival. Where actual practice rather than mere book learning is emphasized, where religion, philosophy and spirituality are not separate from one another, where knowledge and love, reason and devotion, are never divorced from each other, there does the truth of authentic nonduality effloresce.

Historically speaking, experiential Advaita originated with the ancient Rishis. Therefore, the Upanisads contain the nondual truths of the Vedas which declare: idam mahabhutam anantam aparam vijnanaghana eva, *"This great Being is endless and without limit. It is a mass of indivisible Consciousness only."*

SRV Associations & Universality

The SRV Associations are part of a worldwide movement of spiritual aspirants devoted to the study and practice of Vedanta and Divine Mother Wisdom. The ideals of this ancient pathway to God, exemplified in the lives of Sri Sarada Devi, Sri Ramakrishna and Swami Vivekananda, are the original and eternal perfection of the Soul and its inherent oneness with Reality, the manifesting of divinity in our lives, selfless service of all beings as God, and reverence for the ultimate unity of all sacred traditions. To this end our purpose is to study, worship, and contemplate Truth so that spirituality may flourish. This is the Advaitic way — *"None else but Self, none other than Mother."*

> With reverent gratitude, we heartily thank the contributing writers of this issue of Nectar of Nondual Truth who have so graciously and selflessly shared the wisdom of their respective traditions and practices.

Nectar's Mission — Advaita-Satya-Amritam

In Sanskrit, amrita, nectar also means Immortality – and this is, indeed, what we are offering: opportunities to become aware of this Amrita that is our very Essence via the rarefied teachings from Vedanta and the World Religions and Philosophies that appear in each issue of Nectar.

Nectar of Non-Dual Truth is SRV Associations' heartfelt offering of highest Wisdom to the human community. It is the sincerest form of love and service we know to disseminate nondual Truth and teachings which transmit pure knowledge, pure love, and true universality. Through Nectar we are working out SRV's mission of spiritual upliftment and education. And for those of us who are devotees of Sri Ramakrishna, Sri Sarada Devi, and Swami Vivekananda, and also students of Babaji Bob Kindler, it is our great privilege to assist in this mission to our capacity. Please join us; this is a universal movement.

Keeping Nectar in Print

Nectar is a free magazine that can be ordered in printed form online at www.srv.org and also viewed online. However, substantial donations are needed every year to maintain this publication in print. Why is this important?

1 – Printed Nectars are best for person to person and organization to organization dissemination of these ennobling teachings that deepen one's own spiritual life and engender knowledge of, acceptance, and reverence for all other paths.

2 – Only printed copies can reach those who do not have access to online viewing, including prison inmates, who are a particular focus of SRV's social seva.

Please Give

Use the subscription/donation form provided at the back of this issue to send a check or credit card payment to SRV Associations, P.O. Box 1364, Honokaa, Hi., 96727. You can also donate online at www.srv.org. SRV Associations is a 501(c)(3) not-for-profit religious organization. Your donations are tax deductible.

Staff of Nectar of Nondual Truth

Publisher
Sarada Ramakrishna Vivekananda Associations
an Annual Publication
For more information concerning the SRV Associations or Nectar of Nondual Truth please contact:
SRV Associations, PO Box 1364, Honoka'a, HI 96727
Phone: (808) 990-3354
e-mail: srvinfo@srv.org   website: www.srv.org
Nectar Subscription is on a donation basis only

No part of this publication may be reproduced or transmitted in any form without permission from the publisher. Entire contents copyright 2013. All Rights Reserved. ISSN 1531-1414

Editor
Babaji Bob Kindler

Associate Editor
Annapurna Sarada

Production
Lokelani Kindler

Acknowledgement
*Image of Ramakrishna's Disciples
Courtesy of Vedanta Press*
800-816-2242

Cover – Prakasha Ben Cavalcanti

Contributing Writers
Swami Aseshananda
Swami Brahmeshananda
Swami Sunirmalananda
Dzogchen Ponlop Rinpoche
Sheikh Nur al-Jerrahi
Rabbi Rami Shapiro
Rabbi Eli Mallon
Professor Sharad Chandra
Professor Edward Ulrich
David Escobar
Paravasta Sam Bailey
Babaji Bob Kindler

EDITORIAL

   With the incomparable blessing of the principle of Universality as our underlying foundation and confirmed philosophical perspective, Nectar of Nondual Truth and its staff launches into its twenty-eighth issue, every one of them dedicated to the truth of Nonduality, or Advaita, as it appears in all of the religious traditions of the world.

   Like previous offerings, this issue of our one-of-a-kind religious magazine has a rich store of wisdom teachings contained within it. One only has to turn to any of its many pages to find a glowing testament to the Truth and its veracious expression through so many illumined vehicles. In this regard we humbly offer our gratitude to the enterprising writers, authors, teachers, and practitioners who generously contributed both time and wisdom towards this positive outcome. Though this work of religious and philosophical egalitarianism may not reflect it outwardly, it is quite a task to find even a small host of open-minded individuals to share essential parts of their respective traditions in a congenial manner in this day and age. That it has been accomplished, and will continue to be, is valid and substantial proof that the spirit of Universality is alive and well in the world. Both care and effort must be taken in the future to ensure that it will never die out.

   The most popular of all editorials nowadays is that one which is controversial, radical, and challenging of other perspectives and opinions — in short, which invites vociferous contest and highlites variance of opinion as its only point. But I am not interested in popularity, nor in disputatious conflict, but rather in the promotion of a unique spiritual life-giving message that finally puts to rest, even to death, "that self-serving spirit that is the mother of all dissension." Advaita, or Nonduality, is that revivifying message, lending itself most effectively to a sweet and welcome disencumberment that is the sole and timely herald for all-out Freedom. As Gaudapada states in his famous and ingenious commentary of the Mandukya Upanisad:

   "Nonduality is the highest Reality; duality is spoken of as its modification. Even though the dualists lay out their various conclusions, they all contradict each other. In the indisputable Truth-view, called Ajativada (birthless, deathless pathway) there is no contradiction, and it maintains no conflict with other views. In those for whom duality exists, Advaita has no conflict. The Dvaitans may rush to prove the origination of the unoriginated, but tell me — how can an unborn Verity pass into birth? The immortal does not become mortal, nor does the mortal become immortal. How can there ever be a change in one's essential nature? It is only in appearance that the unborn Advaita becomes modified, feigning so through the powers of its own Maya — not otherwise, under any circumstance. If It were to become modified, the immortal would go the way of the mortal! How can an Entity that is immortal by nature go to mortality, unless by artificial means? It remains changeless, and unmoving. As to the three stages of philosophy, with their beginning, medium and advanced levels of insight, the Shruti allows for them out of compassion."

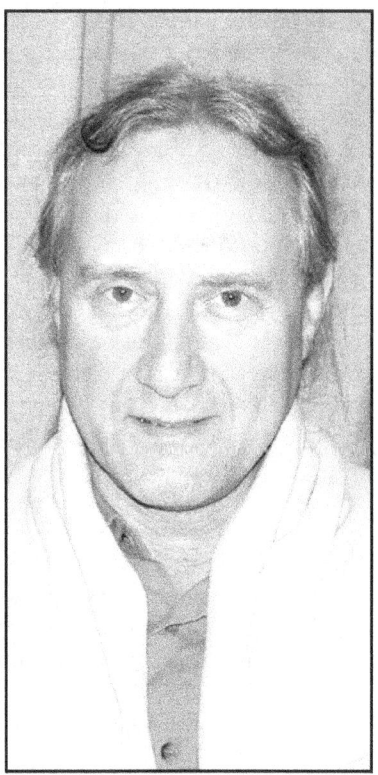

   This is the best of India, and a philosophical Ideal that would be worth living and dying for — if life and death were real. As it is, Advaita is the essence of Eternal Life. Thus, the "Truth-View" is to be heard of from the lips of an illumined preceptor, then studied with full attention, digested over time, and finally realized. At this prime juncture it must be brought full circle and exemplified in everyday life, in full view of one's family, society, one's friends, and one's students. There should be no place where the halcyon Light of Advaita Vedanta should not reach or go. This is the decree of Swami Vivekananda, the harbinger of uncompromised Nonduality in this day and age — to whom this issue of Nectar of Nondual Truth is duly dedicated. Over the 150 years since his advent, the West and the world, what to speak of Mother India, have experienced a positive transformation the likes of which have not been seen since the spread of Buddhism around the world in early times.

   Let the high-minded articles in this issue express and reflect the superlative axioms that Advaita Vedanta is based upon, then, inspiring all those who would storm the gates of Absolute Reality in intrepid fashion.

   Peace, Peace, Peace.   *Babaji Bob Kindler*

Nectar of Advaitic Instruction

Questions from Our Readers

Life in relativity, with all its many challenges, is dealt with directly and efficiently via the process of question and answers brought forth from the minds of the sincere seekers within the salubrious atmosphere of holy company. This is life in the dharma, which swiftly transforms relativity into the radiant realm of Reality, and neutralizes the poisons of relative existence. leaving the mind pure, free, and able to pursue the purpose of human existence — *"....enlightenment of the entire being, including all its passionate intensities."* With this in mind, and utilizing this precious tool called "Atma Vichara" in Vedanta, the intrepid spiritual wayfarer embarks upon the adventure of Consciousness, exploring every bit of matter, inspecting every thought in the mind, studying every facet of Divine Reality that will convey upon him/her *"The Peace that passeth all understanding."*

"I am reading the best book I have ever read so far — The Gospel of Sri Ramakrishna — and thank you for the suggestion. I can understand why it is an initiation prerequisite. As far as I am into the book, Sri Ramakrishna makes many distinctions between the devotional path to God as practiced by the Bhaktas, and the wisdom/reasoning path of the Vedantist. When he describes both of these paths he breaks it down to bhaktas finding God through devotion and intense love of God's forms, while the Vedantist practices the reasoned path of 'not this, not this' to find God in Its formless nature as within one's own consciousness. My question is this: Is there an alternative to reasoning one's way to God without having to use 'not this, not this' as a mantra? The reason I am asking is because I see the world as such an intrinsically beautiful place that I would rather say 'I am That,' or something of that nature.

Sri Ramakrishna speaks about the different paths for the devotees, but He really wants that intrepid devotees, of a more special class, integrate both paths — wisdom and devotion. So blend wisely your devotions with your neti neti discrimination. You will find that they complement one another famously, with very good and positive results.

As per your question, the *neti neti* method is classic, and time honored. I think that you need not look for another wisdom method, but only look deeper into neti neti and then change your attitude around it based upon more time spent with it and more study in it. Yes, at first it seems rather stark, monastic, even sterile; but all that is only outer appearance. In truth, and to the one who is ready and qualified, it accomplishes what other methods only promise to do, but always fail. And remember, *neti neti*, "not this, not this," is based upon arriving at *iti iti* — "all this, all this." The process is only a weeding of the garden of the mind so that real food can grow there, real nourishment. Give it a good chance to do its right and proper work. In the meantime you can say *"Sarvosmi, Sarvosmi!* — Everything Is" — while neti neti practice takes away all that is unreal and detrimental to your life of the Spirit, and from life in the world.

Another bit of helpful teaching is that a mantra (seed syllable in accord with the names of God), and a Mahavakya (Great Saying), are used differently. The former is repeated many times a day, while the latter is uttered only once in a while. Both are to be meditated upon. Pertinent to your question here, the mantra is connected with God with form (Ishvara), thus Bhakti Yoga, while the Mahavakya is tied to God beyond form (Brahman), or Jnana Yoga, generally speaking.

"We were reading the Katho Upanishad last night, and had a question. Yama is discoursing on reigning in the senses. We are wondering what is the process of reigning in the emotions. Do emotions stem from attachments to the senses?

At first, the question seemed contrary to me, as you are using the word "reigning" to mean drawing back, when it really means holding office — like the "reign" of a king. Then I realized you meant the word "rein," like the reins that Sri Krishna holds in His hand on Arjuna's chariot. We certainly do not look forward to the "reign of the senses." Really, otherwise. We want their control.

So, with this little correction, I can state that reining in the emotions is similar in function, especially given the condition of people in the world today, and particularly in the West. Yes, the emotions do attend upon the senses and their experiences, and also follow them around in the case of an uncontrolled mind. But that word, "mind," is more to the point here. The mistake in the common run of thinking today is to assign the emotions to the heart rather than to the head. It is in the psyche where emotions have their seat. The Atman is the heart, and it does not need controlling; it needs realizing. We definitely want the "reign" of the Atman over every other thing, thought, and principle. Then, the base emotions will have no sway or influence. So if you control the mind, you control emotions.

There is a case to be made for emotions that are refined. Here, with inner work and practice, emotion can transform into devotion, and that can be used to realize God/Atman. Passion, which is connected to emotions, should be made to run the route of dispassion leading to compassion. There you have a refined set of emotions emerging. That is the gist of it, and you can now run with it in discussion.

"Thank you for being patient and sincere with my questions on shamanism. They've led me to another question, one in the vein of alchemy, about the coincidence of opposites. How does this pertain to the Vedanta? And is it an Advaita or Dvaita paradigm? Is it wise to acknowledge the apparent existence of pain and ecstasy (such as the event of childbirth or death)?"

Pairs of opposites, always conflicting with another, definitely fall into the realm of duality, and thus, to the Vedantist, are unreal and to be forborne as long as the embodied condition lasts. We do not believe in them as 1) being real in and of themselves, and 2) constituting the true nature of Reality. These dualities, called by the Father of Yoga (Patanjali) dvandva mohena, or "deluding pairs of opposites," can and are to be transcended via one-pointed concentration and the practice of meditation. In daily life they are only to be watched from a detached witness perspective. They are the nature of both (ordinary) mind and relativity.

As to your final question, yes, it is very wise indeed to heed the pairs of opposites — not, as I wrote above, as being ultimately real — but as pointers, indicators, teachers, even friends; for duality, or Dvaita, if it be based in states of God-realization (lower samadhis), can be a very rich tradition, just like Shamanism and others. It really all boils down to the quality of any given individual's particular state of consciousness at any specific phase of time. In other words, it is all in the mind, and I mean this to say that if the western psychologist tells you this about your nonconventional experiences, then he usually means that they are illusory — a figment of your imagination. But if a luminary tells you this, he means to say that they are all a projection of your mind, and real for as long as that very mind perceives them, but not afterwards, when it attains nonduality, or samadhi.

So, meditating upon pleasure and pain, and birth and death (and life as opposed to Eternal Life), is a very healthy way of seeking Truth. Embrace the pain that it brings too, and the sobering of the mind — its waking up from so many dreams, fantasies, and meanderings of the mind in maya. And do not forget to go further and meditate upon the subtle-most dualities as well, ones like form and formlessness, void and nonvoid, existence and nonexistence, and bondage and liberation. These in particular will lead one to the Absolute Existence of "What Is," or "Who am I."

"If you would be so kind, how does being in a state of coma relate to deep sleep?"

A brief answer to your question runs, that the state of coma and deep sleep have at least one thing in common: that the consciousness has disassociated from the physical body. However, in coma (I would think), there are many experiences still going on in the psyche (dreamlike ones), whereas deep sleep has put an end to all those, and to the forms that occupy them. Thus, deep sleep is authentic formlessness, but with effect missing; the cause (to embody) is still potential, however. This distinction between deep sleep and dreaming (and comatose experiences) is beneficial to contemplate, as is the difference between deep sleep (sushupti) and samadhi (Turiya).

One other thing should be added: the consciousness of a person in a comatose state also probably slips in and out between dreaming and deep sleep. The interesting teaching around this is of the "silver thread." It is a subtle nadi that holds the transmigrating soul fast to the physical frame. If it be severed (in the case of the yogis) or is severed at the time of death (of an ordinary soul), there is no further return to the old body. Life, once thought real (in the case of the ordinary soul), then takes on the dreamlike state, and whatever state the transmigrating soul can thereafter manage (based upon its grade of realization in life/waking state), that is where it is — i.e., ancestors, celestials, Indraloka, Ramakrishnaloka, etc.

So, a little further, the comatose state is not a good one for spiritual growth. About the most that can be accomplished, other than returning to normal consciousness, is for the stranded soul to break the silver thread and depart the body. And even here, the state it goes to will be dependent upon its past karmas — positive, mixed, and negative. The seers teach, then, that it is on earth where karmas are formed (bondage) and broken (liberation), and that the state of "heaven" one goes to will be based upon how one lived on earth.

To place this in Vedic perspective, dreams only reflect what one has previously done in the waking state, and dreams will only become radiant pointers towards Reality (as in visions of Mohammed, Peace be upon Him, or Ramakrishna, Bliss be upon Him) when the waking state is mastered.

In short, none but the illumined souls move outward from deep sleep to the dreaming state to the waking state free of restrictions and in knowledge of the oneness of these three states of consciousness. Others partition them out of ignorance. To quote the Para-Brahma Upanisad in this regard, "The ignorant soul imagines the three lower nadis/states to be separate, and thus wanders in bondage. The aware soul, gaining wisdom from the Vedanta, does not suffer delusion from the three lower states, realizing the oneness of all four of them."

"I would like to ask a few questions regarding the ten cosmic powers of the Maha Shakti. About a month ago, I went to a yoga camp in the Carpathian basin. There we learned a lot about the forms of the Divine Mother, the goddesses Kali, Tara, Chinnamasta, Dhumavati, Matangi, Bhuvaneshwari, and Tripura Sundari. In this study, each deity has a symbolic identification to Brahman, and this is to be seen in Prana, which in different qualities and quantities, vibrates throughout the galaxies in everything. We also learned that every physical aspect of the Ishta represents a specific fulfillment, which is mastered through the meditation on that certain form. In certain teachings it is said that it is beneficial and acceptable to look upon Kali or Krishna as a friend, an existing form which, in deep meditation or in prophetic dreams, speaks to you and uses his or her weapons to defeat demons and move about and act. Is this something that really exists in a different realm, or is it just symbolism which is used for meditation to realize the nature of Brahman?"

Nothing happens at all except in and through the mind. No world or loka exists on its own, but only exists in the mind. This is true of the physical world as well. To put it in a nondual way of saying, there is no world that is independent of Brahman. As Swami Vivekananda states, *"Brahman is not in the world, the world is in Brahman."* In this vein he continues:

"Gold and silver have I none, but what I have I give to thee freely, and that is the knowledge of the goldness of gold, the silverness of silver, the manhood of man, the womanhood of woman, the reality of everything is the Lord. And that this Lord we are trying to realize from time without beginning in the objective and in the attempt throwing up such 'queer' creatures of our fancy as man, woman, child, body, mind, earth, sun, moon, stars, the world, love, hate, property, wealth, etc.; also ghosts, devils, angels and gods, God, etc. Herein lies the secret. Says Patanjali, the father of Yoga: 'When a man rejects all the superhuman powers, then he attains the rain cloud of virtues.' He sees God. He becomes God, and helps others become the same. This is all I have to preach. Doctrines have been expounded enough. There are books by the millions. Oh, for an ounce of practice!"

Notice the constant objectifying, and the "queer creatures of our fancy." It is all projection by the mind. Remember, that the mind has not only its individual aspect, but its collective and cosmic aspects as well. When Christ talked about the "Kingdom of Heaven within," and "My Father's Mansion has many Chambers," he was speaking of the Great Mind — Mahat. It is Eternal (deathless). It is Intelligence (Consciousness). It is saturated with and flows from The Word, and that Word is the medium for Brahman and Shakti.

When you ask about Mother Kali, that is Shakti Supreme. The Dasamahavidyas are aspects of that Divine Mother. We are to come to know Her in meditation after the study of scripture and japa of Her name of the mantra given to us by our Initiatory Guru — The Mantri Guru. Sri Ramakrishna is the Shambhavi Guru; He is superlative and incomparable. He and Sri Sarada are the manifestations of Mother Kali in this age. You are extremely fortunate that you have taken birth under a father who has a deep dharmic connection to Them. Now the lineage falls to you. How will you utilize it?

To finish answering your question, gods and goddesses — as well as ancestors, celestials, etc., are in different realms, called Lokas (or Spandas, or Akashas), but one should not imagine that these are outside of oneself, or even out in elemental nature. There exists a form of nature that is subtle and unseen, an Unmanifested Prakriti, that shapes all the inner worlds, and these are existing in Consciousness and consisting of Intelligence. One's dreams are carved out of that. Think of it. When your five gross senses turn off in sleep, five subtle senses ignite and cast forth light, lands, liquids, love, and living beings whose numbers remain untold.

And in fact, it is all symbolism in a sense, i.e., symbols, objects, forms, along with their respective names and designations, combined in time and space, and animated by cause and effect — it is all Maya. It is all as unstable as a lone bean in boxcar, as shifty as a rattlesnake on fire, as evanescent as a marshmallow in a dream, and makes about as much sense as "the son of a barren woman." Only Brahman is real, so the wise keep their minds focused on That. *"They conquer all who conquer Self,"* as you quoted.

In Brahman there are no worlds; the worlds are in Brahman. Formlessness is just what it says it is. Otherwise, there would be no such words like samadhi, satori, and nirvana. So when these forms arise, know that it is all the mind's business. And when it comes time to deal with all these forms, and put them away, it becomes Shakti's business. Chinnamasta will sever the head of ignorance, Dhumavati will burn all form to ashes, and Tripura Sundari will reveal to Her devotee what lies beyond the triple aspect, what is most precious and most hidden.

"Secondly, at the yoga camp I got to look a bit into Yantra meditation. It seems like an exciting thing to meditate on. Can Yantra, via visualizing, focus the mind on a God or Goddess, like a Mantra? What are the differences compared to a Mantra? Would it be acceptable to use? I also heard that there is to be a new Avatar who will live at the end of the Kali Yuga, who will help to harmonize the world once again. His name, according to the yoga school, is Kalki. Is this information valid, or is just something to forget about?"

As for Yantra and its practice, that is about as symbolic as philosophy and practice can get. For those who cannot envision deities, or who have no attraction to them, the diagram (salagram, yantra, mandala) provides a point of focus that, though it at first seems mathematical and geometric, is really only an illustration in the physical of the infinite dimensions lying within Consciousness. In each of those spaces (three-sided, for it takes three lines to enclose a space) lie subtle realms, and therein exist the deities of differing aspects. We do not see them here, unless they become embodied for some reason (like the Avatar). They exist in subtle space, and that is where our earthly sense and scientific conception of height, width, depth, breadth, and manifold dimension fails to inform us. The particle is vibrating in maya; The Word is vibrating in Reality.

As for the future Avatar, Kalki, He is described in tradition, so what can one say? But our point in Ramakrishna tradition is that there is much left to still unwrap from all the Avatars who have already come to us. So, we ought to focus there and learn what they have taught, and not get caught up in projections around the future. Otherwise, this is like the case of the man who comes out of the shower looking everywhere for his towel, overlooking the fact that it has been lying across his shoulders all the while.

"If everything, including different heavenly realms, are projected and created by the mind, then why is it that animals, plants, and geographical scenery were not designed by the human mind? These things were here before the human being existed on the face of the earth. Or is it that it is OM that creates everything, and that Brahman still vibrates in everything, including our thoughts, being the omnipresence of all worlds?"

Who said that animals, plants, planets, etc., are not projected by the mind? In truth, these things could not preexist the noble human being, who is author of the universe. To the Truth-knower, God, Brahman, Divine Reality, is not a Creator; we leave God (Brahman/Reality) out of the productive/destructive equation (It is Acreate), and instead try to realize "That" beyond name and form — which It is.

> "Creation (projection) is not without repercussions. The ability to dissolve, therefore, is just as if not more important to know about and wield than that of formulation. Therefore, know and love Brahma and Vishnu, for sure, but do not forget to worship Siva!"

As the rest — all that forms in space and time due to cause and effect — we must not overlook the existence of Consciousness. Man is Consciousness first and foremost, and a name and form producer and participant in his own creation after that. It is only when he forgets his own Consciousness that he errs, falls into primal ignorance (mula-vidya), and begins to think of himself as bound, limited, a product of nature, and other silly concepts.

For higher understanding, then, you will have to get beyond the historical frame of reference to comprehend that everything, including plants, animals, land — earth, water, fire, air, and ether — is all fabricated by the Mind (cosmic, collective, individual). When man thinks in terms of a mere historical reference, he remains a slave to time. When man thinks in terms of origins, he becomes a slave of appearances only, of beginnings, middles, and ends — of maya. Man, especially God in mankind, was present long before the five elements came together to shape various forms in nature. If you are origin-bound, then read your Bible if you will (God breathed upon the waters), but make sure to read it in the clarifying Light of the Upanisads. And consult Swami Vivekananda as well.

When Swamiji states that God is not in the Universe, but that the Universe is in God, what do you think he means? All comes from Consciousness; where else would it come from? Nature? Nature is insentient. How can it be the author of anything. It is a mere matrix. It is a plant, insect, animal and human body producing machine, but every mechanism has got its inventor. The Mundako Upanisad states it clearly: *"Anterior to life and mind is the Atman."* How can it all be a matter of time, when time is illusory? All of time exists in the Eternal Moment. All of space exists in the subtle-most spiritual Ether. And that moment and that space is going on in you eternally.

And you come closer to realization when you bring in the Word, AUM. It is the medium for all form. Its reverse side is the doorway into Formlessness. Why is it that an illumined Yogi will hear the sound of AUM in meditation? Because It is within him, and it is the source of power through which he projects, sustains, and withdraws worlds of name and form in time and space. He is careful to remain free of cause and effect, however, using such subtle force carefully and with sensitivity. Creation (projection) is not without repercussions. The ability to dissolve, therefore, is just as, if not more, important to know about and wield than that of formulation. Therefore, know and love Brahma and Vishnu, for sure, but do not forget to worship Siva!

Productive power lies in the head. Beings devoid of this knowledge project all manner of oddities — fantasies, imaginations, speculations, conjectures, ideas, thoughts. It is called Sankalpa and Vikalpa in Sanskrit. Do they think that these forms of thought-energy do not have karma attached to them? That they can just catapult them out of the uncontrolled and uninformed mind without suffering the results in some way, in some form, at some time — near or distant?

The result of such unknowing is what we see around us in the form of confusion, randomness, indeterminacy, heedlessness, and other negative forces of the human mind, unleashed upon a world which, as a result, suffers ignorant, evil, vile, and violent actions. Can we not trace all these to the mind? Have they come from insentient nature? That nature displays its own awesome destructive powers such as floods, earthquakes, fires, and the like is only a direct indication that all these bits of extraordinary phenomena proceed out of the ever-pregnant and potentially volatile mind of the human being — which also contains the ancestors, gods, goddesses, etc. In it rests all that is benevolent and malevolent. Thankfully, Brahman resides beyond it.

And you are correct when you say that Brahman infills everything. But It does not vibrate; the Word does all that. And via Shakti, all energy, from Kundalini on through to various levels of thought-force and prana, animates the many worlds. Thus, the Source and the many phases of Origin ("In the beginning was the Word") are different ("the Word was 'with' God") up until the human being attains to Samadhi ("and the Word 'was' God").

Therefore, the great words of Christ and other luminaries were spot on; they just need a fresh and original interpretation, accompanied by a quick departure from the gross interpolations and text-torturing of holy scripture that has gone on over many centuries.

"Can you tell me what happens in the Sushumna Nadi during an orgasm? What happens energetically to the Kundalini coil during this time?"

The physical experience people have in sexual relations is a kind of ecstatic moment, a slight tremor of the root chakra, when subtle energy momentarily activates the Ida and Pingala and one can get a sense of the flow of spiritual energy from one center to another. It gives one some glimpse of the light and bliss that are a result of Kundalini awakening. Unfortunately for most, the experience itself overrides the meaning and potential of it, and all its greater significance gets overlooked.

And it is not only this grave oversight that is disappointing, but physical attachment often results as well. In many cases, anger follows. Lust and anger have always been close companions in the human mind. Many misconceptions and false teachings spring up and surround the experience as well. The entire branch of Tantra concerning it has thus been corrupted and is considered a lower teaching, potentially dangerous to the aspiring aspirant's bid for candidacy for enlightenment.

"So much is made, in New Age thinking, of cultivating the ability to manifest the fulfillment of our desires. When I read about the 'laws' they are utilizing, such as: 'Our thoughts create our reality,' it sounds almost Vedantic. In these Raja Yoga lessons, we are also learning how we will ultimately conquer nature and verge upon omnipotence. However, only the yogi/yogini who has achieved a spotlessly pure mind and has ascended to a very high state can claim that 'everything comes to him/her naturally.' This seems to run counter to our precept of renunciation, that we are meant to give up the world, not seek to satisfy our desires in it. I find it ironic that once we approach the pinnacle of spiritual life we may receive omnipotence, and yet in order to reach our ultimate goal, we must give it all up. In the meantime, as spiritual beings apparently associating with these physical minds and bodies which are naturally filled with desires from sunup to sundown – aside from the obvious risk of being overly distracted by worldly attainments – is there anything wrong with utilizing certain powers of thought projection to manifest a more comfortable life for ourselves and those we love? In other words, spoken from a truly western perspective: Can I renounce my cake and eat it, too?"

Words like "comfortable" are red flags in the spiritual world, among the gurus and preceptors. The tendency to compromise the truths of the scriptures, to misinterpret the real meaning and import of renunciation, and to prevaricate around one's spiritual practice, is all too common, especially among the western peoples. If one were to manifest a more austere life, that would be lauded by the knowers of Truth. Why do people always think in terms of comforts, and not see the value of renunciation? The former breeds bondage, the latter leads towards freedom. Renunciation builds character, and that is what strengthens spiritual life. Pleasure and comforts, praying for and manifesting all that you want, only short-circuits spiritual life, contrary to popular thinking.

The expression, "New Age thinking" is a contradiction in terms. For the most part they do not think, these world lovers, these sentimentalists, these believers in birth and death, these materialists masquerading as enlightened persons. Buddha thought; Christ thought; Shankara thought. These are the true luminaries, and they did not own a stitch or covet a thing. They said, respectively: *"Suffering Is"*; *"Birds have nest, foxes have holes, but the son of man hath no place to lay his head." "Everything, from unmanifested nature on down to the element earth — it is all the nonself."* If these are the world's true luminaries, and these are their words, then does it behoove the seeker after Truth to seek, own, and covet the things of this world?

So, I say, along with them, use the powers of your mind to put an end to mental projection — called sankalpa/vikalpa, imaginings in time. Live in the world as a turtle does, who swims in the waters of the ocean but keeps its mind always on its eggs buried in the sand. If one can do this, all preparation is made — for contentment, for peace of mind, for bliss, for ultimate freedom. And prior to the arrival of all these, desires will get satisfied naturally.

Sri Ramakrishna has used the analogy of a rich man's country mansion. It lies uninhabited for months, with little or no activity taking place in it. But one can know of the zemindar's coming for a visit when all of a sudden there is a flurry of activity, with many servants moving a host of furniture and eatables into the place. The master is about to arrive. Just so, when qualities like contentment, peace, and subtle bliss attend upon the aspirant, it is not long before enlightenment itself will make its appearance. And the preparation for this is not longing for wealth, or goods, or pleasures, or comforts; it is longing for God, for Reality Itself. The more desires and possessions one has, both in one's life and in one's mind, the further away will Divine Reality keep Itself.

So, if one truly wants freedom, and has tasted it so that one knows a little of what it is, and what it actually feels like, manifest in your life the desire for desirelessness — nirvasana. Be content with contentedness. Even if you have home, spouse, possessions, etc., do not own them; do not even think about them as your own. Renounce them daily, if you have to. Even the custodianship of these, though it teaches many lessons, eventually turns onerous. The one final lesson it teaches is "I want none of this, only freedom." As our priceless eternal friend, Swami Vivekananda has put it:

Have thou no home. What home can hold thee friend?
The sky thy roof, the grass thy bed,
and food what chance may bring,
well cooked or ill; judge not.
No food or drink can taint that noble Self
which knows Itself.
Like rolling river free thou ever be, Sannyasin bold!
Say – "Om Tat Sat Om."

Is there a compromise, or a halfway measure in all of this for the nonmonastic temperament? I think not. The householder must be more on his/her guard than the monk who is already courting freedom. Otherwise, the insinuation of maya comes full bore, destroying spiritual life and undoing the fiber of inner character outright. Before one knows it, lands, wealth, relationships, children, pets — all of life weighs like chains on the soul. To quote the luminaries, it is all empty, lacking in real substance, constantly changing, permeated with suffering, and will ultimately turn sour. Renounce it all now and save yourself much suffering later. People may think, "I can enjoy it now, and later easily give it up." But these shortsighted beings are not accounting for the subtle onslaught of habit, attachment, complacency, and the sapping of inner strength over time which a life of insouciance results in.

Moreover, what to speak of compromise, turn it all into Brahman's manifestation. Why manifest things for oneself? Leave it as it is, Brahman's already perfect manifestation, and enjoy it all immensely without the bindings of ownership and personal agency, ever free of the mind's urges towards creating more. One must live like a sword — constantly cutting away, never accumulating for long. Beautiful! Beautiful! this life of well-tended freedom, this superlative view of inner terrains, this rare breath of spiritual heights. Let us never risk spoiling it with mental or physical clutter. As Sri Krishna advised Arjuna, *"Be content with anything."*

> "One must live like a sword — constantly cutting away, never accumulating for long. Beautiful! Beautiful!, this life of well-tended freedom, this superlative view of inner terrains, this rare breath of spiritual heights. Let us never risk spoiling it with mental or physical clutter. As Sri Krishna advised Arjuna, 'Be content with anything.'"

"I liked hearing about the 'pranic bubble' and would like to know more about how that connects to the concept of the 'cosmic egg,' or Hiranyagarbha. Is that referring to the same thing, or is the first on an individual level which succeeds the latter? It brings back the wonder of how the One becomes the many, and our discussions on the juncture of the seer and the seen."

The pranic bubble, as we call it, is a facilitator for the rebirth of the as yet unrealized soul and its return to the realms of gross name and form. Really, it can be discarded as of no further use after enlightenment has dawned, for if there are no contents (of the mind) then there need not be any container.

Put another way, a higher form of prana, leading up to Shakti power itself, becomes the facilitator, and takes refined consciousness to deeper levels of awareness for experiences that fully transcend all the gross worlds of name and form. Anthropomorphically, this refined carrier is exemplified by the presence and form of Garuda, the great dragon bird, that carries Vishnu on many flights (of wisdom) to various inner realms. The swift speed of this primal mount far outstrips the slower movements of the gross or ethereal prana, which itself is much faster than the speed of light here on earth. The Tantracists call this "manojavittvam," the speed of the mind and its thought. People of this technologically advanced but spiritually benighted age would be well served to take stock of this subtle energy that transports the mind in microseconds to higher states of awareness, and brings it back to a perception of grosser things as well. Sound familiar? It is samadhi with its ebb, flow, and recession. Controlling the mind is all about this too, is it not?, as well as controlling the prana.

So forget the cartoony dragon birds of Hollywood and get ahold of the real Garuda. Then, instead of fantasy flights (sankalpa/vikalpa), you will experience the lightning fast rise and fall of spiritual moods too numerous and blissful to count. Enough of dangerous forays into physical sky and the thin air of open spaces. Try inward ascension and swiftly reach the goal of human existence.

"I find it most helpful to think of the elements as states of existence, but could you please elucidate what it means for air to be aligned with "homogeneity?"

In the way that I am using it here, homogeneity is the mode of being everywhere, like water or air, while not permeating objects — like an island resisting an ocean or a mountain dividing the overall body of air. All-pervasiveness is the word I have chosen for something that interpenetrates everything, like ether with planets; it is not only around them, but it shoots through and through them as well. And so, by analogy, we see that air represents mind/intellect, while ether represents Atman. As referring to the tanmatras, which you infer here, air's subtler component is the idea of homogeneity in the mind of God. That is where air came from, starting out as a Word/Thought and finally, after a substantial trickle-down process, congealing on the physical level as the element we call air.

Lord Buddha gave us another way to think of the five elements. They are the five types of desires of living beings. This perspective gives even more validity to the "mind-only schools" way of thinking, which propose to us that the universe is not created out of nothing (nothing doesn't exist!), but comes forth via the thought processes of masses of beings existing in various lokas at cosmic, collective, and individual mental levels. Thus, earth has five forms (akashas) and so do the other four elements. Water at a subtler level is the flow of prana. Fire at a subtler level is the light of intelligence, etc.

Further, what brought them forth practically and cosmologically is different from, but intrinsically linked to why they came forth, which is also linked to who brought them forth. The "why" is desire, and the "who" is the mind/ego complexes of tamasic, rajasic and sattvic beings. Over the course of this great Cosmic Projection, "who" got the desire to ask "why" (or "why not"), and projected the "what" some "where" "when" it willed it. Thus the Five "W's" came into being. Unfortunately, the "Who" has been discarded in these times for the other four "double U's" (two selves instead of one), and people are thus unaware of the Self (Who) and fixated with why, what, where, and when — i.e., cause and effect, matter/objects, space, and time, respectively. When they begin seeking answers to their dilemmas, or even question deeply at all, their queries are invariably wrapped around and hung up in these inferior modes.

In short, and with regards to desire, kama, mankind wanted a solid place to "lay his head" (big mistake!) so he projected earth (with the help of mind, maya, and nature, a little invisible help of shakti power); he desired to drink, to enjoy, to generate, and quench, so he projected water; he yearned for radiance to light up the solid and subtle worlds so he projected fire; he longed to move freely, to be warm and cool, to fill and empty, so he projected air; and finally he desired to transmute between worlds of his own design and choosing so he projected the ethers — all from the abundant power inherent in his own mind on three joint levels.

Whatever else may be said about the power inherent in mankind — and there is plenty — desire is no doubt a powerful thing and must be watched with care. As long as the desire for dharma precedes the desire for a world of five elements, we are okay. Lose the dharma, however, and we ourselves are lost.

Questions, observations and insights regarding the issues of the day or problems in spiritual life may be directed to Nectar's editorial staff at srvinfo@srv.org and will be duly addressed in succeeding issues.

◆ *Swami Sunirmalananda*

SURVIVAL OF THE FITTEST
LIVING FULLER LIVES

Man, particularly the selfless man, outlives all others — because in service he truly lives, renouncing all for the sake of others. Such a being lets go of the object and beholds the Eternal Subject. In this regard, Swami Vivekananda wrote: "The fact is that the Lord is in us, we are He, the eternal subject, the real ego, never to be objectified, and that all this objectifying process is mere waste of time and talent. When the soul becomes aware of this it gives up objectifying and falls back more and more upon the subjective. This is the evolution, less and less in the body and more and more in the mind — man, the highest form, meaning in sanskrit, manas, thought — the animal that thinks, and not the animal that senses only."

Survival of the fittest has become a popular phrase. Herbert Spencer coined it in 1864. Darwin used it to mean "Natural Selection." The idea that the fittest alone will survive on this planet has gained sufficient ground thanks to Darwin.

Nobody lives forever, but the idea is that those who are the fittest will survive, while others succumb to pressure and pass. Even Swami Vivekananda has said that Nature appears to favor the fittest: "*According to the law of nature, wherever there is an awakening of a new and stronger life, there it tries to conquer and take the place of the old and the decaying. Nature favors the dying out of the unfit and the survival of the fittest.*" (4:377). But Swami Vivekananda is speaking here about the tendency of the new to replace the old — newer forms trying to replace older ones.

Hail, the Physical!

Who are the fittest ones? What does fitness mean? Remember, there is this superlative — the fittest ones. Is it physical fitness? At least in the physical world it appears to be so. In our everyday world the fittest alone appear to survive, while those who are unfit have always succumbed to difficulties. This is what appears to have happened throughout history to plants and trees, animals and birds, individuals and groups, institutions and nations — the physically weak have readily made place for the strong. History always repeats the story of how the weak have been smothered out. Further, medicine also seems to proclaim that if you are strong you can avoid ailments and infections. One does not require Socrates to prove that the world we live in is one of challenge, competition, and constant struggle. If we are not fit enough to face the world and its challenges, we perish. So the simple truth is, to survive in this world, one should strive for physical fitness.

"But a Small Germ Can Kill a Massive Elephant"

So far so good. But is this the unimpeachable rule? There is, on the other hand, that remarkable statement from Swami Vivekananda: "*They talk a great deal of the new theories about the survival of the fittest, and they think that it is the strength of the muscles which is the fittest to survive. If that were true, any one of the aggressively known old world nations would have lived in glory today, and we, the weak Hindus, who never conquered even one other race or nation, ought to have died out; yet we live here three hundred million strong!*" (3:156).

Just as there are countless cases like Hercules overpowering Nemean lions and Mares of Diomedes, and Supermen doing impossible things, there are also cases of the physically weak surviving relentless attacks. So, physical fitness, though necessary, is not everything for the simple reason that we are not just our bodies. The body, with all its network of muscles, is not sentient on its own, and needs something else to keep it going. This body is not the real "I," though many of us live as if it is, some even taking recourse to corrupt and unethical means to satisfy the body's demands. Man is not like other animals, struggling only for the upkeep of the body. His life proves that physical strength is not everything. Ailments, problems, and difficulties come to even the strongest of us, and is thus a case in point.

Finances of the Fittest

What is fitness then? Financial fitness? Perhaps. Some seem to decide that the fittest are the rich, those with a healthy bank balance. In other words, if you have money, you can have anything. That is the popular idea. The present-day consumerist society fully endorses the idea that money means fitness to survive. However, not all rich beings are really surviving, despite flexing their muscles of money. While the poor go on surviving somehow, the rich seem to always need more to live by.

Coming to nations, financially fit countries do not appear to be happier than impoverished ones. Though millions of souls may drag higher ideals down to satisfy their lower desires, and though even the most sublime thoughts and ideals may get misused only for physical and monetary benefits by the masses, the fact remains that neither the body nor possession of money can bring true fitness to humanity.

Therefore has India, since time immemorial, glorified the ideal of having less, of owning little. This is called renunciation. To survive, therefore, does not mean merely to breathe, eat and make oneself financially strong. This philosophy may hold good at the animal level, but at the human level only a life of peace and dignity will suffice. Animals and other creatures may survive physically by being strong, but the human being needs a dif-

> "While those who lived for themselves might have conquered continents and sat on prickly thrones placed inside pools of blood, worrying constantly about their enemies, those who have conquered their desires and ambitions have lived in peace and stability."

ferent type of fitness to survive.

Surprisingly, this unique fitness is exactly the opposite of what is commonly understood by the word "fitness." As was said, the popular notions of fitness are physical and economic health. That is, generally, to survive, we think it should e "me" first. But to survive in the truest sense of the term, one needs the ideal of "me" last, and others first. *Vairâgya mevâbhayam* — renunciation alone brings true peace. We should be able to say, "you go first."

For instance, Swami Vivekananda once wrote to an Indian prince, one who knew fully well what physical and financial fitness meant: "*My noble Prince, this life is short, the vanities of the world are transient, but they alone live who live for others, the rest are more dead than alive.*" (4:363). St. Francis of Assisi sang the same tune when he said: "*It is in giving that we receive, and in dying that we are born to eternal life.*" So the fittest, the noblest, and the bravest are those who sacrifice for others, and they alone survive.

Appearance and Reality

Is this possible? Isn't it contrary to facts? While history appears to show how the physically strong and the powerful seem to always survive in the ordinary sense of the term, it also shows clearly, time and again, that it is the selfless alone that have truly survived in this battle of life. It is really not the rich or the supermen, but the apparently ragged and weak ones who have been the most successful. While those who lived for themselves might have conquered continents and sat on prickly thrones placed inside pools of blood, worrying constantly about their enemies, those who have conquered their desires and ambitions have lived in peace and stability.

Those who lived for others alone have attained the goal of true survival, which is attaining inner peace. How could survival mean attaining peace, you may wonder? When someone falls into a blazing fire but comes out unscathed, he or she has survived the fire. Just so, those fittest of the fit who have lived for others, have lived in peace, acquired immense merits owing to their selflessness, and have attained supreme good. They have not survived like vegetables, living until death arrives, but have lived the fullest of lives and transcended death. They have not survived like animals, living only for satisfying the basic desires of the body. What is more, even plants and animals are seen to live for others, while we humans cheat, lie, and hate to please ourselves. But this can change.

The selfless ones are different: they live like the gods. Their names are sung longer than time can imagine. To survive in this sense not only brings inner fulfillment but also keeps the body in shape, the mind in order and peace, and the heart filled with happiness. The anxiety that is involved in trying to survive the ordinary way is worse than death, and so people take to corruption and other means to compensate. As Swami Vivekananda has written, "*Anxiety is worse than the disease.*"

Fitness and Practicality

When all is said and done, living for others is fine. But we must also survive in this world. In this present age we shall also have to take care of ourselves and our families. How can we combine selflessness with our own welfare? Should we only ignore our family and go about doing good to others? This is where the genius of Vivekananda comes in. He knew what struggle means, having suffered the tortures of the world immensely in his younger days. He therefore presented the ideal of Karma Yoga, the way of working so as to serve God in mankind and thus live every moment of our lives fully. He valued renunciation, *tyaga,* but also knew that India's ideal was equally about service, *seva*. As a result, thousands of people all over the world are now practicing these ideals, and are leading excellent lives.

Who are the truly fittest then? On 18 February 1902, Ramakrishna's birthday, Swami Vivekananda wrote to Swami Brahmananda: "*If in this hell of a world one can bring a little joy and peace even for a day into the heart of a single person, that much alone is true; this I have learnt after suffering all my life; all else is mere moonshine.*" He also once said: "*I can secure my own good only by doing you good. There is no other way, none whatsoever.*"

Swami Sunirmalananda is a monk of the Ramakrishna Order, who has served its branches in Belur Math, Mayavati, and Brazil. He is now Assistant Minister at Centre Vedantique, Geneva.

Many Happy Returns

The mother's heart, the hero's will,

The softest flower's sweetest feel;

The charm and force that ever sway

The altar fire's flaming play;

The strength that leads, in love obeys;

Far-reaching dreams, and patient ways,

Eternal faith in Self, in all

The Light Divine in great, in small;

All these, and more than I could see

Today may "Mother" grant to thee.

— Swami Vivekananda

◆ Dr. Sharad Chandra

SWAMI VIVEKANANDA
& His Women Disciples & Friends

Swami Vivekananda's life was like a dazzling flash of light dispelling darkness around it. He lived a total of 39 years of which the first nineteen were no different from the carefree life of any extra-active, energetic, restless, young man — in his words, an "unsympathetic, uncompromising fanatic." Yet records exist to impress that, notwithstanding his tempestuous and unmanageable nature, he was given to solitary contemplation, social service, and charity right from his childhood. At the age of twenty-one, Narendranath Dutta, as he was known before taking his monastic vows, got himself initiated into Freemasonry on February 19, 1884. Around 1881, at 19 years of age, he was in Dakshineshwar, meditating deeply under the guidance of Sri Ramakrishna Paramahamsa, and could access samadhi. In July 1890 he set out on his pilgrimage to the Himalayas, and in the last week of January 1891 began his two-years' travel in India to know his vast country and its people.

During this journey Swami Vivekananda lived with all kinds of people — the lowly and the outcaste, sweepers, thieves, prostitutes, as well as the upper caste pundits, rajas, and maharajas. He saw misery and suffering at first hand, which caused him many sleepless nights. This experience widened his outlook, broadened his moral vision, and made him realize the difference between relative truth and Absolute Truth. These were the years of his apprenticeship, so to speak, and also of what may be called the formative years of his preceptorship. This is when he formed his close relationship with the Raja of Khetri, Ajit Singh, accepted disciples, and initiated the deserving into monastic life.

This is also the time when he became conscious, more than ever, of the spiritual wealth of his motherland and his consuming need to do something for the poor. The thought crossed his mind that *"the whole world had need of India."* The health of India, and the impending death of India, was also his concern as well. At this juncture, as if by divine inspiration, a pandit in Porbander advised him to go to the West where he would be better understood, and where he would be able to find means to eradicate poverty at home. The idea instantly reinforced the plan already taking shape in his mind. He started looking for a way to go to the West. In the autumn of 1892, he heard of a Parliament of Religions to be held in Chicago the following year. His immediate thought was how he might take part in it. By February 1893 he made up his mind to go, and proclaimed it publicly in Hyderabad in his lecture, "My Mission to the West."

Go West, Young Man

Swami Vivekananda arrived in Chicago in late July of 1893, wishing to represent Hinduism at the Parliament of Religions. But he was totally unknown in America, and also unequipped, lacking any kind of credentials. Even back home he was known simply as a specially gifted disciple of Sri Ramakrishna, the *"comfort of his soul,"* his only disciple whom he regarded as his *"other self."* Since the Parliament of Religions was scheduled to open on September 11, he was left with the need to find lodging and support himself in a strange land for several weeks. At the suggestion of a well-wisher he took a train to Boston where, he was told, the cost of living was lower. It was in the train from Chicago to Boston that he met *"an old lady"* who invited him to live at her farm house, "Breezy Meadows," in Metcalf, Massachusetts, not far from Boston. It was through this lady that he met Professor John Henry Wright of the Harvard University. At once appreciative of Swamiji's spiritual prowess, he persuaded him to return to Chicago and attend the Parliament of Religions. Prof. Wright made all necessary arrangements and also took it upon himself to introduce Swami Vivekananda to the West as a highly qualified delegate.

This was the beginning of Swami Vivekananda's ascendancy in the West. Many people were influenced by his message and his life during his stay. Women were specially attracted toward him. Undoubtedly they were mesmerized by the charm of his dynamic personality, impressed by his knowledge and oratory, but they were also highly qualified, intelligent, intellectually gifted, and spiritually thirsty souls in search of truth, and that was the reason of this immediate bond. They were themselves great, and that is why they could recognize greatness in him, could feel his presence, talk intensely about him, and discuss spiritual topics with him.

Western Women Disciples

A large number of men and women became his disciples and devoted friends. Women especially played a central role in his life and work. From these American women — each remarkable in her own way, and all of them Christians — he received deep friendship, love, reverence, and support for his work. They opened their homes for him. To some he was like a son, to others, a brother full of love and fun. His heart was full of admiration and deep gratitude for them. In January, 1884, he wrote to Raja Ajit Singh, *"Last year I came to this country in summer, a wandering preacher of a far, distant country without name, fame, wealth, or learning to recommend me — friendless, helpless, almost in a state of destitution — and American women befriended me, gave me shelter and food, took me to their homes, and treated me as their own son, as their own brother."* He was a great letter writer and wrote to most of his friends and disciples. His letters to these American women show how close he felt to them, and how much he valued them.

With the women he met in London, or elsewhere in Europe,

> "Women especially played a central role in his life and work. From these American women — each remarkable in her own way, and all of them Christians — he received deep friendship, love, reverence, and support for his work. They opened their homes for him. To some he was like a son, to others, a brother full of love and fun. His heart was full of admiration and gratitude for them."

it was the same story. A close relationship of mutual love and reverence always sprang up. Some organized lectures for him, arranged meetings and retreats centering on spirituality as preached by him, while others found and rented rooms so that he could hold classes on practical Vedanta. At the end of his lecture they would freely discuss with him their doubts and apprehensions about the new religion. Swami Vivekananda enjoyed these meetings and appreciated their interest and curiosity. Most of them later became his devoted disciples. The reason behind such response on both sides was a spiritual outlook and a common search for truth. Of these extraordinary ladies, Miss Katherine Abbot Sanborn, Margaret Noble (later known as Sister Nivedita), Josephine McLeod, Sarah Ole Bull, and Mme. Marie Louise (later Swami Abhayananda), deserve special mention, and also, Christine Greenstidal (Sister Christine), and Mrs. Charlotte Sevier, his "American mother."

The story of Swami Vivekananda's life is inseparable not only from that of Sri Ramakrishna Paramahamsa, primarily, but also from these women of the West who became central to his life and work. It is not possible to understand Swamiji's personality, his philosophy and vision, his concept of practical Vedanta, his views on education and human development, without knowing more about these devoted women, their work and writing on Swami Vivekananda, and their reminiscences of him.

Katherine Abbot Sanborn, the good-hearted lady who lent support when Swami Vivekananda had just landed in Chicago and didn't know a soul, was a well-known author who had taught at Smith College. She most graciously invited him to live in her house in Massachusetts.

When he stayed with her he did not know that in the vicinity of Boston there lived another woman, Mrs. Sarah Chapman Ole Bull (1850-1911) who would become one of the greatest supporters of his work, his guide in practical matters, and his emotional anchor. A deeply spiritual person, she recognized straightaway the depths of the Swami. She had read the *Bhagavad Gita* translated by Mohini Mohan Chatterjee. Her husband was a great musician and their home was a centre of sparkling intellectual conversations.

In the spring of 1894 she invited Swami Vivekananda to be her guest in her home at Cambridge, and also invited her philosopher friend, William James (1842-1910), to meet the Indian monk. Subsequently, William James and Swami Vivekananda kept meeting off and on over time. There is no written record of those conversations, so nothing definite can be said, but the author's *The Varieties of Religious Experience* (1901), and *The Psychology of Religion* (1902), do reflect much of what they most likely discussed. Sarah Chapman (Mrs. Ole Bull) donated liberally to the establishment of Vedanta societies in America, and gave one hundred thousand rupees for building the Belur Math. More importantly, she gave him her unlimited love and care and a sensitive understanding of his inner sufferings. It is to her that he turned not only in matters pertaining to the organization, but also for rest and peace. In his customary manner he gave her a Sanskrit name, *Dhir-mata*, the steady mother.

Madame Marie Louise was a French woman who met him at the Thousand Island Park retreat organized by Mary Elizabeth Dutcher in the summer of 1895 for a select few. She was later initiated into Sannyasa by Swamiji and was given the name of Swami Abhayananda.

A later woman devotee of similar name was Marie Louise Burke (who later came to be known as Sister Gargi). She was the disciple of Swami Ashokananda who came to America and taught in San Francisco at the Vedanta Society. Marie Louise's detailed research on Vivekananda in the West, spanning more than half-a-century, enables us to know him more vividly through her work, by knowing more about those who came into his life, and whose lives he entered. Her classic six-volume work, *Swami Vivekananda in the West: New Discoveries*, may be the most authoritative work on him to date. Marie Louise Burke lived till as recent as the 20th of January, 2004, when she passed away in San Francisco, aged ninety-three.

Margaret Elizabeth Noble was in her late twenties when she first met Swami Vivekananda on November 10, 1895, at the house of her friend, Lady Isabel Margesson, who had organized a session in her house in London for her selected friends so that they could listen to Swamiji. In her search for truth, at once compelling and agonizing, Margaret Noble had moved restlessly from one faith to another, from one knowledgeable person to another, including George Bernard Shaw and W. B. Yeats, but her soul's longing still remained unquenched. She loved Jesus with her whole heart, but found the fundamentalist Christian doctrines incompatible with Truth. Indeed, she found the salvation preached by Buddha decidedly more consistent with the Truth than the preachings of the contemporary Christian religion in England. It was during this quest that she met Swami Vivekananda, heard him, and asked him questions after each talk. By the time Swamiji was to leave London she was calling him, "Master." She then dedicated her life to the subject most dear to him: the education and emancipation of women in India.

Just as Margaret Noble was the greatest gain of Swami Vivekananda's first visit to London, Captain Sevier and Mrs. Charlotte Sevier were those of his second visit. Josephine McLeod has written somewhere that once, Captain Sevier, coming out of the hall after hearing one of the lectures by the Swami, asked her skeptically, "Do you know this young man? Is he really what he seems?" Her one word answer, "*Yes*" carried such con-

> "He said something, the particular words of which I do not remember, but instantly to me that was Truth; and the second sentence he spoke was Truth, and the third sentence was Truth. And I listened to him for seven years, and whatever he uttered was, to me, Truth."

viction that the Captain made up his mind then and there, saying, "In that case one must follow him, and with him find God." The Seviers eventually sold everything they had in England and came to India with Swami Vivekananda when he returned home in 1897. With their money they built the Advaita Ashram at Mayavati in Almora. Dying in Almora three years later, Captain Sevier never saw England again.

Variously called Joe, Joe-Joe, Yum, and Tantine, Josephine MacLeod was one of Swami Vivekananda's closest friends. Tall, attractive, and wealthy, she had an imperious air about her. She heard Swami Vivekananda for the first time in January, 1895. The effect it had on her can be best expressed in her own words: "He said something, the particular words of which I do not remember, but instantly to me that was Truth; and the second sentence he spoke was Truth, and the third sentence was Truth. And I listened to him for seven years, and whatever he uttered was, to me, Truth." She joined his entourage and remained with him till the very end. She believed Swami Vivekananda to be the new Buddha. On being introduced as Swamiji's disciple, she immediately shot back, "I am not Swamiji's disciple; I am his friend," to which her niece, Alberta (later Lady Sandwich) added, "She is not Swami's friend. She is him." She used to refer to Swamiji as "our prophet." When Josephine MacLeod met Mrs. Sarah Bull, there grew between them a bond of unwavering love for each other, of their shared love for "our prophet," and of the togetherness of making his message of Vedanta known even more widely. To this duo was added a third, Margaret Noble. With a twinkle in his eyes the swami would often refer to them as "The Trinity."

One story goes, that a day before the Parliament began, when Swami Vivekananda arrived in Chicago, penniless and hungry, he was walking casually in the streets. Suddenly a woman emerged from a house and asked him, "Sir, are you a delegate to the Parliament of Religions?" On learning that he indeed was, she took him inside her home, gave him breakfast, got his luggage from the railway station, and took him to the offices of the Parliament where, of course, he was awaited. This lady was Mrs. Ellen George Hale. Later the whole family — she, her husband George, her two daughters Harriet and Mary, all became his good friends and supporters. Of all the families he came to know in the West, the Hale family always remained the dearest to the Swami. He described their house as his "domestic monastery," his personal "Math."

In comparison to these many western women disciples, very few names come up in India — actually just two: Mrinalini Bose and Sarala Ghoshal. His letters to them were formally addressed to "Dear Mother," and "Dear Madam," respectively, and lack his characteristic wit, playfulness, and the warm informality with which he wrote to 'My dear Joe-Joe' (Josephine Mcleod), or to 'My dear Babies' (Misses Harriet Hale and Mary Hale and their cousins), to 'My dear Frankincense' (Mr. Francis Leggett), etc.

They were both educationists and he expected them to work for the emancipation and education of women, the two issues he himself worked passionately for. Mrinalini generally followed Swamiji's directions, but Sarala Ghosh did not seem to respond.

In more contemporary times, a third person in India whom I have found completely devoted to his vision, is Pravrajika Atmaprana, known mainly for her biography of Sister Nivedita. However, her long article, "Swami Vivekananda on the Harmony of Religions" found in the Vivekananda Centenary Memorial volume (1963), is no less enlightening.

Go West Again

Swami Vivekananda went to the West on a second visit in June, 1899, and spent most of his time on the West Coast of America. After delivering many lectures there, he returned to Belur Math in December, 1900. The rest of his life was spent in India, working incessantly for his ideals of practical spirituality, service of the poor, education and emancipation of women, and the harmony of religions. His health began to show signs of deterioration toward the end of 1901, and the end came quietly on the night of the 4th July, 1902. More than a monk, he was the consummate and innovative sannyasin, a dynamic personality, and a fiery soul. His words had a magnetic effect on the life of those who heard him. Today, he is not here in person, but his words and deeds continue to inspire people all over the world.

Dr. Sharad Chandra is a former University teacher turned full-time writer, editor, and journalist. Her several awards include the Grand Prix from Academie Francaise, Paris, and the Dwivagish Samman in India. She has been a Foundation Gulbenkian, a Minister of Culture, and is also a French Scholar. At present, she is the senior resource person for the Culture and Value education workshops.

Professor Edward T. Ulrich ◆

EARLY CHRISTIAN ASCETICISM

The "Conferences" of John Cassian

There is a longstanding criticism of Hinduism in the West as being too otherworldly and impractical. Christianity was and often continues to be considered a strong contrast to this, as being oriented towards this world and hence as contributing to the development of modern science and similar accomplishments. Labeling and categorizing other peoples and their ways is often a means of defining one's own identity and role. For instance, this generalization about Hinduism served colonial purposes, for it implies that Indians were incapable of governing themselves, that they needed an outside government.

Western scholars in recent decades began debunking many ideas about Hinduism which served colonial purposes. They began doing this mainly by considering Hinduism in its wide variety, rather than assuming a particular school or branch to be normative. However, in addition to this one could examine more closely the party that has made the myth. For instance, one could raise the question of whether Christianity has always been as practical as it is today, if it has always been so focused on this world.

Before exploring this question, this essay will point out a few reasons why many people believe that Christianity contributed to practical aspects of the West today. First, some believe that the Bible helped set the stage for the emergence of modern science with its doctrine that God created the world and saw that it was good, which contrasts with the doctrine that the world is an illusion, maya, to be dispelled. Also, Jesus' concern with the poor seems to be an inspiration behind some of the civic institutions which exist today in the West. Further, the image of God in the Bible as a personal reality who directly intervenes in the affairs of the world gave a strong sense of duty to some groups to work hard in the world and transform it according to what they believed the will of God to be.

In spite of all that, one might doubt that Jesus fits standards of practicality common in the West today. For instance, he was an itinerant preacher with no permanent home, saying of himself that *"the Son of Man has nowhere to lay his head"* (Mt 8:20, Lk 9:58 New Jerusalem Bible). When his family approached him to bring him home he denied that they were his true family and claimed his followers as his family (Mk 3:31-35). When he saw his followers fretting with cares he told them that they should not worry about tomorrow. Instead they should trust that God will take no less care of them than the birds of the field and the lilies of the valley; he feeds the former abundantly and ornaments the latter lavishly through their feathers (Mt 6:26-28, Lk 12:23-27). Further, he preached that the end of the world was near and that people should live in constant expectation of this (Mk 13:1-37). Finally, he walked freely to the city of Jerusalem, knowing he would undergo a gruesome death there (Mk 10: 32-34).

Although Hinduism was and has been criticized by some Christians as too otherworldly, in the ways shown above Jesus was little different from a classic sannyasin. The sannyasin gives up his possessions and family in order to continuously wander the countryside. Further, he does not store up food but trusts to the generosity of others by begging. Finally, a sannyasin might elect to quietly sit under a tree, absorbed in meditation, not taking food or water, until the body wastes away and dies. The scholar will point out significant differences between this death of a sannyasin and the death of Christ, but both were voluntary and impractical by worldly standards.

Christ's impractical spirit continued into the first centuries of Church history. For instance, after his death his followers led a communal lifestyle, holding all their possessions in common (Acts 2:44-45; Cassian Conferences 18.5.1). In fact, the Bible reports that two would-be converts, Ananias and Sapphira, dropped dead when they were confronted for keeping some of their wealth to themselves (Acts 5: 1-11; Cassian Conferences 18.7.1). Later, as Christianity spread across the Mediterranean, it earned the scorn of Roman intellectuals for its belief that the Godhead, who is eternal and unchanging, became a human being, Jesus Christ. Also, converts caused discord and heartache within their families by refusing to follow traditional ways and customs. Last, but not least, some Christians would go to their deaths for refusing to worship the emperor, even when they were asked to give only a small gesture of worship for the sake of conformity to the law.

In the early fourth century Christianity was legalized, the persecutions ended, and by the end of the century it had become the dominant religion of the empire. Although many in the Christian community were elated by this change in fortunes, many also regretted it, for the moral standards became lax with a large membership. Longing for the zeal and fervor of earlier days, some Christians separated themselves from society, retreating to the deserts of Egypt to follow the morally rigorous lifestyle of earlier days. Leading celibate lives and having isolated themselves from their families these people came to be known as "monks," coming from the Greek word monachos, meaning "alone" (18.5.3-4).

John Cassian (365 [?]-435[?]) gave one of the main accounts of early Christian monasticism in his Conferences. He lived as a monk and wandered the deserts of Egypt, gathering the teachings and stories of elders, revered monks, referred to today as the "desert fathers." He later traveled to the West, settling in what is today France. There a different lifestyle was taking root, cenobiticism. Various hermits, given the severe difficulties of living in solitude, gathered together to live in a loose group context. This lifestyle was different from that of the hermits in Egypt whom Cassian reported about, but he transmitted the wisdom and experiences of these hermits to the cenobites of Gaul; he was a conduit from East to West.

According to Cassian, the heart and center of monasticism is prayer. Cassian considers a variety of prayers uttered by Jesus in the New Testament, and he considers the "Our Father" as one of the best of prayers (Mt 6:9-13). It contains seven requests or petitions, each of which is focused on spiritual realities, not material. The first petition is that the name of God be "hallowed." Cassian explains that the monk should pray that he will glorify God's name, hallowing it, through a life of moral purity. The next two are that God's "kingdom come" and that his "will be done on earth." God's reign has not yet been established on earth as a whole, but his reign can be established in individual hearts and the monk prays that this will happen in his own heart. The next petition, that God give us our "daily bread," is a reminder to the monk that there is no progress on the spiritual path without God's grace and assistance. In brief, the "Our Father" is simple in nature, containing seven petitions for spiritual realities, not worldly things (9.18-9.23).

Prayer is the heart and center of monasticism, but it is hard for the mind to stay focused on God. Cassian relates a way of drawing the mind back to God, a way that would have a deep impact on Roman Catholic and Eastern Orthodox spiritualities. One should recite over and over in the mind the following verse from Scripture: "*O God, incline unto my aid; O Lord, make haste to help me*" (Ps. 70:1, quoted in Cassian Conferences 10.10.2). The monk uses this prayer to keep drawing the mind away from distractions. In that way it is like a *mantra* from Hindu tantric traditions. However, while the tantric mantra has power by virtue of its sound, which is sacred, the prayer Cassian recommends is efficacious through its meaning. It reminds the aspirant of his dependence on God and the fact that he is always present, ready to offer assistance (10.10.3-4). Cassian advises that this verse "*....be the first thing that comes to you when you awake, let it anticipate every other thought as you get up, let it send you to your knees as you arise from your bed, let it bring you from there to every work and activity, and let it accompany you at all times*" (10.10.15).

The goal of such attentiveness to prayer is to reach a level beyond all concepts of God. In this state one does not pray by the "*sound of the voice or a movement of the tongue or a pronunciation of words.*" Instead, through an "infusion of heavenly light," prayer "*gushes forth as from a most abundant fountain and speaks ineffably to God*" (9.25.1). Cassian states that this was the nature of Jesus' prayer when he would withdraw alone to the mountains and when he was waiting in the garden of Gethsemane before his arrest.

Solitude is essential for the high levels of prayer to which the monk aspires. To explain this Cassian compares the human soul to a feather. A feather will fly up into the air with a puff of wind if there is nothing to burden it. However, with even a sprinkling of water the feather is earthbound. Likewise, a pure mind will easily ascend to contemplative heights, but burdened with worldly concerns and vices the mind cannot soar (9.4.1). It is in solitude that one can find freedom from worldly cares and one can pursue the necessary moral rigor. Cassian draws the reader's attention to the example of Jesus, who would withdraw from the crowds to the wilderness to pray. It was not necessary for Jesus to be alone to pray, but he withdrew nevertheless in order to set an example for other humans (10.6.4). (Although considering solitude to be essential, Cassian was not espousing the total solitude of the classic sannyasin. For instance, while the sannyasin may eschew the common rituals of Hinduism, Cassian's monk continues to participate in some of the rituals of Christianity.)

One should avoid promptings to rouse oneself from solitude. These include, perhaps surprisingly, even the desire to perform acts of charity, to become a priest, and to help lead others to God. The monk must consider all these desires as sinful, and they are particularly troublesome because they appear as holy desires. Cassian explains they are like coins that appear to be from the king's mint, bearing his image, but are in fact counterfeit. If one gives into such desires one's stability will begin to falter and one will eventually abandon the monastic path (1.20.4-8).

Although considering solitude to be essential for deep prayer, Cassian has serious reservations about some motives for renunciation. For instance, there are those who give up the world to escape from the responsibilities of managing household problems and earning a living. Such escapism is identifiable by the fact that the so-called monk will not submit to the authority of an elder monk or follow established monastic customs (18.7.3). Another motive for solitude is to conceal one's faults from others; if one has limited contact with others one can put on a show of moral perfection. However, Cassian warns that "*the more it [a vice] is concealed, the more deeply the serpent works an incurable disease in the sick person. Virtues are begotten not by hiding one's vices, but by fighting them*" (18.8.2).

Having introduced Cassian's system, one can return to the question of whether Christianity, in contrast to Hinduism, is very practical in nature. Christian critics of Hinduism often consider the school of Advaita Vedanta, which teaches that distinctions between one's deepest self, the Atman, and the ultimate reality, Brahman, are false. There are a wide variety of Advaitic schools, both ancient and contemporary, but Advaitic schools generally teach that the ultimate reality is beyond words and forms. Further, a classic belief is that to realize the unity between Atman and Brahman one must become a sannyasin renouncing one's social and familial ties. Some traditions have taught that the sannyasin must be completely solitary. For these reasons, Advaita is often labeled as "acosmic."

One might wonder if John Cassian was any less world denying than many Advaitic traditions. To begin, he aspired to a state of prayer beyond all words and forms. Furthermore, he considered solitude to be essential to experiencing this wordless, imageless state. In fact, he went so far as to discourage charitable acts if they meant leaving the solitude of one's cell or of the local monastic community, considering it to be sinful to do so. Hence, it would seem that he was as acosmic as many Advaitic traditions. Cassian was very different from the latter, in that he aligned himself with the emerging orthodox position in the churches, which endorsed a dualistic relationship with God. However, this fact does not negate the overlap which exists between Cassian and Advaita.

Recognizing the overlap between Cassian and Shankara, but nevertheless still wishing to criticize Hinduism for its otherworldliness, one might question Cassian's status in the Christian tradition. Was he a marginal figure, perhaps significant in earlier centuries but later abandoned? The solitary lifestyle of the deserts eventually faded out and in place of it developed the communal lifestyle of monasteries, in both the Roman Catholic and Eastern Orthodox churches. However, the spirituality of Cassian had a deep impact on monasticism, and monasticism in turn had a significant impact on European history. The monasteries played, and continue to play, important roles as centers of culture, learning, stability, and spirituality. Hence, although the lifestyle of the desert fathers is gone, Cassian's spirituality has an enduring significance.

A further, worthwhile point to consider is that the acosmism of Cassian and Shankara was qualified by an awareness of the importance of a variety of roles in society. To consider this matter in Cassian one must first turn to St. Paul's First Letter to the Corinthians, where he discussed the dynamics of the Church as a community. Different members have different gifts, such as healing, prophecy, and speaking in tongues. There is a hierarchy among these gifts, some being greater than others. However, all gifts are important for the task of building up the community, just as all parts of the human body are important for its proper functioning (1 Cor 12:4-30, 14:1-5).

Drawing on that idea, Cassian stated that there are a variety of routes to perfection. While some might choose solitude others might choose a life of charitable acts (14.4.1-14.5.1). The important issue is that, having chosen one's path, one stick to it and persevere. In his words, *"It is impossible for one and the same person to shine simultaneously in all the virtues that I have listed above. If someone wants to strive after all of them together, in his pursuit of them he will of necessity not possess a single one completely, and he will suffer loss rather than make gain....For there are many ways that lead to God, and therefore each person should finish the one that he has taken up"* (14.6.1).

There is a similar approach in the Bhagavad Gita, which is a key text in Hinduism's classic philosophical traditions of India and is a popular text today. Whilst St. Paul wrote about the importance of a variety of roles in the Church, the Gita considers society as a whole. There are different social groupings, known castes (which might have been significantly different from today's caste system), each of which has its allotted duties. When members of each caste perform their respective duties society, and the world as a whole, function well. At the beginning of the Gita, Arjuna, the famous warrior, would like to withdraw from the world in the face of an impending battle, for relatives of his belong to the opposing army. In the face of his reluctance, Krishna explains to him that although renunciation and meditation constitute the highest path, Arjuna must remain in the world and fight the opposing army, carrying out his duty as a *kshatriya*, a member of the warrior caste. Members of each caste can attain the highest reality by focusing on their respective societal duties, but they must focus on them in a spirit of detachment from the world and devotion to *Ishvara*, their Chosen Ideal (Bhagavad Gita 1.28-47, 2.47, 2.54-3.30, 18.41-62).

Although St. Paul and the Gita recognize the importance of a variety of roles there are wide divergences between them. For instance, St. Paul was addressing the operation of the Church but the Gita considers the functioning of the society as a whole. Further, the Gita was reinforcing existing social groupings whereas St. Paul was trying, in certain regards, to eliminate social divisions. These differences are significant but they do not belie the important parallel between Paul and the Gita, the parallel being the recognition that a variety of roles are essential to the whole, and thus, in the case of Cassian a qualification of his acosmism, and in the case of Hinduism, a qualification of the acosmism of some Advaitic traditions.

To conclude, just as one should not essentialize Hinduism, reducing it to just one form, neither should one essentialize Christianity. Today, Christianity seems to some to be a practical religion focused on this world; it has not always been this way. As discussed herein, Jesus lived a lifestyle of self-abnegation and many early Christians followed his example. Also, many of the early Church fathers, including Cassian, were influenced by the philosophy of Plato, which considers this world a realm of delusion and our true home to be in a non-material intellectual world. This otherworldly focus continued in the West through the Middle Ages, and scholars believe that a variety of factors diminished it over time, some of these factors having been the rediscovery of the philosophy of Aristotle in the 1200s, the Italian Renaissance in the 1400s and 1500s, the Protestant Reformation of the 1500s, and the influence of the Enlightenment in the 1700s and subsequent centuries. The river of time cannot be reversed, for it flows ever on, but Christians should look back to earlier sources, like John Cassian, expanding their notions of what Christianity is and has been, and seeking spiritual nourishment from these early sources.

Edward Ulrich is an Associate Professor of theology at the University of St. Thomas, where he has been teaching since 2000. His courses are "Introduction to the Christian Theological Tradition," "World Religions," "Hinduism and Buddhism," and he also brings students to India. He is currently researching the nineteenth century Bengali social and religious reformer, Keshab Chandra Sen.

◆ *Swami Brahmeshananda*

PILGRIMAGE TO PAVAPURI

The Sacred Atmosphere of Jainism and Lord Mahavira

Our series on Jainism continues unbroken into its seventh straight issue, as Swami Brahmeshanandaji describes his pilgrimage to Pavapuri, the site of Lord Mahavira's Nirvana, in exquisite detail.

My trip to Pavapuri, the Jain tirtha or sacred place, where the twenty-fourth and last Jaina tirthankara, Lord Mahavira, attained nirvana, had been much delayed, and when I finally reached there on the sixth of November, winter had just set in. A village in the State of Bihar, Pavapuri is situated fifty-nine miles southeast of Patna and fifty-four miles northeast of Gaya. It is nine miles from the nearest town, Bihar Sharif, and is located on the Bakhtiyarpur-Ranchi national highway.

Passing along the western and the northern banks of the lotus lake and then through the village, the jeep carrying me reached a place called Samavasaran. It had two temples with an annex of Dharmashalas or inns for pilgrims, and was situated one mile east of the main pilgrimage spot, the Jal Mandir. The bus route which skirted along its western and southern compound walls proceeded to a village named Ghosrava. I was put up in a spacious, newly constructed room on the first floor in the southeastern corner of the Dharmashala. There were no electrical fittings and, except for two wooden bedsteads and a mattress and pillow, the room was unfurnished. Although electrical wiring could be seen, Pavapuri had no power supply, but the Dharmashalas had their own generators which they ran for two or three hours in the early part of night. Soon after dusk I realized that the generator was installed just under my room and, apart from making a loud booming sound, it made my room vibrate perceptibly. Except for this nuisance, which I soon learnt to avoid by going to another part of the premises during that period, the room was good. It had windows on three sides. From the eastern window could be seen a small orchard of mango, papaya, banana, and other trees, beyond which were the rice fields. The golden orb of the rising sun could be seen every day. The view of the Rajgir hills towards the southwest was obstructed by a double-story Dharmashala building a hundred feet away.

The place was so quiet that the slightest sound produced at the other side of the inn would be heard as if produced in the adjacent verandah, and at night the rumbling of automobiles plying on the Patna-Ranchi road could be heard distinctly. However, my room was situated so that the noise of visitors and pilgrims coming and going at all hours of the day, and the constant shouts of the caretaker, hardly disturbed me. There was also the tik-tik sound of the chiselling of the marble slabs for the temple under construction: this ceased to be a disturbance once I got used to it. I was provided with a kerosene lantern, a bucket, and a tumbler. Tube-wells provided abundant quantities of excellent water for drinking and washing.

Jain Vegetarianism

Orthodox Jains do not eat after sunset. This rule must be observed by all who stay here. So at five pm I was called by "A," the man in charge of the inn, to dine with him. "A" is a devout Jain who, apart from being a strict vegetarian, does not take even water after sunset, does his spiritual exercise called *pratikramana* every morning and evening, and observes fast or half-fast on the eighth and fourteenth days of the lunar month. I was surprised to learn that he hailed from the Burdwan district of West Bengal, and so we started talking in Bengali, although he could speak Gujarati and Hindi equally fluently. Contrary to my assumption that the Jain population must be thin in the predominantly non-vegetarian Bengal, he informed me that a fair number of Jains lived in many districts of Bengal.

Our conversation over the narrow dining table, which could accommodate only two metal plates, soon drifted to the question of food, partly because, as the person in charge, "A" wanted to know my eating habits, and partly because Jains are very particular about diet restrictions. He was satisfied to learn that I was a strict vegetarian. Much like the "non-touchism" of the nineteenth-century Hinduism, vegetarianism, as an offshoot of the basic principle of Ahimsa or non-violence, has become an obsession with the followers of Jainism. "A" now wanted to know whether eating fish or meat by monks was justified, and whether Swami Vivekananda allowed it. I happened to have some of the works of Swamiji with me. I showed him some relevant passages in which Swamiji had expressed his views on non-vegetarianism. But "A" would not stop even at this. He went on asking whether I ate potatoes and onions. Finally I brought the conversation to a close with a rebuff, "Your religion has been reduced to some regulations and fasting. Instead of thinking about the Ultimate Truth, your people only think of what to eat and what not to eat, and lose your religion if you eat potato or onion." Only once more during my stay was the question of vegetarianism raised, and I used that opportunity to point out to him the exploitation of the poor by wealthy vegetarian Jains. However, "A" like many other Jains who regarded killing of insects as cruel, failed to see the greater cruelty to human beings involved in amassing wealth.

After food, "A" washed clean his metal cup and plate with water and drank the washing, leaving not a particle of food. Later I learnt that this commendable practice was a habit with all cultured Jains.

I soon settled down to a daily routine which included, among other things, going to the Jal Mandir after breakfast, returning for lunch, and spending the rest of the day at Samavasaran. The gates of Samavasaran are closed at sundown.

Hence, except once when I attended the vesper service at Jal Mandir, I avoided being away after dusk. My morning trips gave me enough opportunity to visit and see the various temples.

Jal Mandir

There are six major shrines at Pavapuri. Of these, the most important, most sacred, and most beautiful one is the marble memorial in the centre of the lotus lake at the spot where the mortal remains of Lord Mahavira were consigned to flames. As it is situated in the middle of a lake, this shrine is called Jal Mandir. The artificial lake is approximately 1400 feet long and 1200 feet broad and remains most of the year filled with lotuses. This year, however, lotuses were few, but there were innumerable aquatic birds. A six-hundred foot long and ten foot wide bridge of red stone connects an imposing gateway on the bank to a marble platform in the middle of the lake. This platform, which forms the base of the memorial, is about 120 feet square, having four small domes at the four corners, marble railings on all sides, and steps descending to water level towards the east. In the centre of this square there is a raised platform with steps on all sides on which stands the shrine proper. The shrine faces east and has low entrances on three sides. Inside there are three large niches which serve as altars. On the central altar the footprints of Lord Mahavira, made of black stone and about fourteen centimeters long, are installed. On the two side altars are the marble footprints of his first and fifth lieutenants, Gautama and Sudharma, who succeeded him one after the other as the head of his monastic order. The four domes at the four corners of the outer platform enshrine the footprints of some of the chief apostles, chief nuns, and other saints and Acharyas. The whole structure is built to look like the mythological celestial aeroplane. Pilgrims and tourists are allowed to go to the shrine and offer worship from seven am to seven pm.

Jal Mandir is indeed an extraordinary place. Apart from its scenic and architectural beauty, the shrine has an unusual serenity, and the mind becomes calm and indrawn as soon as one enters it. Here one need not, rather, must not, try to control the mind, but must relax and allow the peace and holiness of the place to permeate one's being.

According to legend, Lord Mahavira spent his last caturmasya (the four months of rainy season when monks do not travel from place to place) at Pavapuri. On the morning of the 14th day of the dark lunar fortnight of Kartika (kartika krsna caturdasi), the last sermon of Lord Mahavir began. Knowing that his end was near, he continued to preach nonstop for 48 hours, what is now known as the "uttaradhyana sutra," until the last quarter of amavasya (night of the new moon) when, as the svati constellation was in the ascendence, he entered nirvana. The gods showered flowers and sang praises. The assembly of devotees, both lay and monastic, were struck with grief, and to compensate, as it were, for the loss of the light of knowledge kept burning so far by Lord Mahavira, lighted innumerable lamps. This is how, according to Jainism, the festival of Dipavali (Diwali) began.

As the news of the passing away of Lord Mahavira spread, people from all parts rushed to have the last darshan of his mortal remains. The body was then carried in a procession to a nearby spot where the last rites were performed. Later on, gods and men, according to their relative status, gathered the sacred ashes into urns and carried them away to be worshiped. When all the ashes were exhausted, people started collecting the holy earth of the spot, and as a result a ditch was formed, which was later enlarged into a regular lake. King Nandivardhana, the elder brother of Lord Mahavira, installed the stone footprints of the Lord at the spot where he had attained Nirvana, and also at the spot where the last rites had been performed. These two places are now respectively the Gaon Mandir (Village Temple) and the Jal Mandir (Lake Temple).

It is difficult to prove the historicity of the above events, for the earliest inscription of A.D. 1203 mentions only a metal image installed by Abhayadev Suri. However, the worn out appearance of the central footprints at Jal Mandir suggest that they must be very old. The other two footprints are clearly of a later date.

The Goan Mandir

The Goan Mandir, or Village Temple, is situated to the northwest of the village and is surrounded by a big Dharmashala. The temple has a spacious hall (nat-mandir) with a dome, the interior of which reminds one of the Dilwara Jain temple at Mt. Abu. The entrance pillars are beautifully carved. Apart from the images of Lord Mahavira and two other tirthankaras, there is a pair of footprints of Lord Mahavira on a high black marble pedestal. According to the inscription, they were installed in A.D. 1588 during one of the many renovations. The original footprints installed by King Nandivardhan are now in a corner, in the same shrine.

To commemorate the nirvana day of Lord Mahavira, a grand festival is held on the Dipavali night when thousands of Jains from all parts of India assemble and offer laddus (sweetmeat balls) at the Jal Mandir, some of which may be as big as 15 kgs each. The festival includes processions, singing of devotional songs, expressing sorrow at the passing away of the Lord, and feeding the poor and the disabled.

The Svetambara sect believes that Pavapuri is also the place

> "The rich Jain community has been pouring millions of rupees on building and maintaining marble temples, but has never paid the least attention to the village. It appeared as if heaven and hell were existing side by side — rich, gorgeous temples surrounded by slums. This is the picture of many Indian tirthasthans, places of pilgrimage. One of the many reasons for this is the common Indian teaching that that one's earnings should be spent first of all for God, then for saints and sages, next for devotees, then for the poor, and last of all for oneself."

where Lord Mahavira delivered his first sermon in 556 B.C., and converted 4400 scholars, Princess Chandanbala, and eleven of his chief apostles, called ganadharas, of which Indrabhuti Gautama was the foremost. He also established the dharma tirtha caturvidha sangha, or the fourfold religious order, consisting of monks, nuns, male lay devotees called sravakas, and female lay devotees called sravikas. Gautama was a Vedic scholar and a ritualist brahmin. He came with his followers to challenge Lord Mahavira but was converted without even a debate. He succeeded Mahavira as the head of the Jains. Some of the teachings of Lord Mahavira are addressed to Gautama, or are replies to questions put to him. It is said that many disciples of Mahavira, even of lesser eminence, and even those brought to the Jain fold by the teaching of Gautama, attained moksa (liberation) quickly, even before Gautama. He, himself, had to wait until the passing away of Lord Mahavira owing to his intense personal devotion to the latter. He had voluntarily preferred to forgo liberation in favor of devotion. To rid himself of this subtle blemish, and to sever the golden thread of bondage, Lord Mahavira sent him on a preaching mission just before he commenced his last sermon. When Gautama, still away, learnt of the passing away of the Lord from the rejoicing of the gods, the hidden motive of the Lord in sending him away at the time of his nirvana flashed in his mind and, freed from the last traces of ignorance, he attained moksa (kevala-jnana) instantaneously.

The Two Samavasaranas

The site of Lord Mahavira's deliverance of the first sermon is situated about one mile east of the Jal Mandir, and is called Samavasaran. But there is yet another place, which also goes by the name Samavasaran, opposite the entrance of the Jal Mandir and across the road. At this latter place there is a mound-like structure which rises in four successive broad tiers, the diameter of the basal platform being thirty-two feet. On the top there is a dome eight feet in diameter containing the footprints of Lord Mahavira on a pedestal. I was told that these were the original footprints which had earlier been installed by King Nandivardhan at the original site of the first sermon. But being away from the village, they were being neglected and dishonored by ignorant people. Hence, these footprints were removed from the original site and installed here. The four broad steps of the mound represent the four compartments of a samavasarana to be described presently. This is called the "Old Samavasaran."

A new marble shrine or monument has been built at the original site of Lord Mahavira's first sermon, one mile away, in 1957. The antiquity of this later spot now called (the new) Samavasaran (where I stayed) is evident from the still standing stupa said to have been built in 526 B.C. The priest of the Samavasaran monument showed me around and described to me what a samavasaran actually is.

According to Jaina mythology, the king of the gods, Indra, prepares an auditorium whenever and wherever a tirthankara desires to deliver a discourse. This is called samavasarana. It is like an enormous cone 35,000 feet high with 20,000 steps, on the top of which Lord Mahavira sits in padmasana under a huge Ashoka tree. It consists of four concentric compartments or galleries. In the topmost gallery sit gods, monks, nuns, and lay disciples. In the next compartment there is a place for birds and animals who sit forsaking their natural fear and hostility. The third compartment is for vehicles and chariots of the gods which, according to Jain mythology, are living entities. The lowermost compartment actually consists of four enormous lakes in which aquatic creatures assemble to listen to the Lord's sermon. The construction of the samavasarana is such that every creature sitting anywhere is able to see the Lord facing him and, through the Lord's divine power, is able to understand the teachings in its own language. Evidently, samavasarana is a symbolic conception of the integral nature of creation and the basic spiritual harmony of the universe.

All the above features are depicted in the marble monument in a miniature form at the 'new' Samavasaran. It is thirty-five feet high and has twenty steps, each step representing one-thousand steps of the original. At the top there are four identical life-size marble images of Lord Mahavira facing the four sides under a big, beautifully carved Ashoka tree. The expression on the face of the image of Lord Mahavira is most sublime. There are three concentric galleries on the walls of which gods, monks and nuns, animals and divine chariots are depicted at their respective places. Below these is a broad terrace with four pits on the four sides which represent the four lakes. The whole structure is most artistic and attractive. As I was staying in one of the rooms of the adjoining Dharmashala, I could see how enchantingly beautiful it looked on moonlit nights.

Thus, the samavasarana is not a temple of the usual type. It is the earthly representation of the celestial ideal of the basic harmony of the universe. Near this marble "samavasarana" a new temple is under construction in which huge (about twice the life-size) marble images of Lord Mahavira, Gautama, and

Sudharma have been installed. There is a remarkable expression of peace, bliss, and compassion on the face of the central, slightly bigger, image of Lord Mahavira.

Other Temples

There are two more Jain temples of lesser importance in Pavapuri. The Digambara Jain temple surrounded by a Dharmashala is situated to the east of the lotus lake. A Svetambara Jain temple is situated opposite the entrance of the Jal Mandir across the road. The Jal Mandir is equally sacred to both the sects, and their devotees offer their worship here.

The Village

My daily walks up and down the serpentine asphalt road leading to the Jal Mandir gave me a refreshing view of the open rice fields spread like a greenish yellow carpet on both sides for miles, with clusters of palm and mango trees standing out here and there. In the last part of my walk I had to pass through the village Puri which, like any other Indian village, is a cluster of mud huts and small brick houses arranged in a haphazard manner. I could see men and women carrying heavy sheaves of harvested rice on their heads, arranging them into heaps, threshing out the grains, picking up the straw, and thatching their huts. In the low-lying area along the road, water had accumulated to form a permanent pond which was used for fishing by the boys of the village and for washing and bathing (Fishing is prohibited in Lotus Lake). A small ill-maintained Siva temple stands on its western bank. There is a primary school with about one-hundred children, a post-office, a branch of Punjab National Bank, a charitable dispensary, and a small medical store selling only some essential allopathic drugs. There is only one telephone in the whole village. There are a number of shops selling articles of day-to-day use. Near the gateway of the bridge to Jal Mandir there are tea-stalls, fruit shops, and booths selling pictures, guide books, and articles of tourist interest. I was told that this village, Puri, is the biggest among the nearby villages, with 400 families. Almost half of the population belongs to the scheduled castes. The village itself is very dirty and the villagers are poor. My physician's eyes detected a number of cases of lathyrism, people walking on the roads with a spastic gait, produced by eating a poisonous pulse called Lathyrus sativus. Owing to the lack of a proper drainage system, waste water from the huts had flowed on the road converting it into a veritable drain. I had to cross this portion of the road by carefully stepping on the narrow raised edge along the side.

The rich Jain community has been pouring millions of rupees on building and maintaining marble temples, but has never paid the least attention to the village. It appeared as if heaven and hell were existing side by side — rich, gorgeous temples surrounded by slums. This is the picture of many Indian tirthasthans, places of pilgrimage. One of the many reasons for this is the common Indian teaching that one's earnings should be spent first of all for God, then for saints and sages, next for devotees, then for the poor, and last of all for oneself.

Since it is difficult to relegate oneself to this rule, the really needy and the poor are the ones who are deprived of a share in a religious man's earnings. Swami Vivekananda has altered this order by raising the poor, the downtrodden, and the sick to the level of gods. I was reminded of an incident in the life of the Holy Mother. A disciple once informed the Holy Mother that Ramakrishna Babu, the son of the late Balaram Bose, the great householder disciple of Sri Ramakrishna, had in his will set apart a large sum of money for the service of the Lord and service of monks. At this the Holy Mother asked him whether he had willed some money to the service of the poor also. This simple incident highlights the new dimension which the advent of Sri Ramakrishna has given to the concept of charity.

A few days later, on meeting R.S., a senior government official of the district, I raised this topic and asked whether something could be done to improve the condition of the village. If the Jal Mandir was the ancient tirtha associated with a departed prophet, the village was the modern tirtha where the living gods in greater need of worship resided. He was of the opinion that unless the villagers themselves took interest it was difficult to help them. Attempts had been made but failed owing to lack of co-operation of the local people. I appreciated the truth of his statement but maintained that though quick results could be obtained if the local people cooperated, in the absence of such co-operation it was still possible to generate such response and change the lives of the people through greater and persistent effort. It was these illiterate, poor, non-cooperative Indians, reduced to the level of brutes by centuries of slavery, that Swamiji especially wanted to be cared for. I requested R.S. to approach the local Jain community, if government help was not available. He agreed to do his best in that regard.

Respect for all Religions

A Hindu monk in ochre robes moving about in a Jain centre of pilgrimage was an uncommon site for the villagers who were used to seeing only white-robed Jain monks. Children ran away from me in fear, women gazed with curiosity from the fields and from their huts, and men gossiped about my whereabouts. On the third day, a group of villagers who had assembled in a shed, approached me as I passed by. After exchanging greetings they asked whether I was going to the Jal Mandir and was staying at Samavasaran. When I replied that I was, they took me to be a Jain monk and asked why I was dressed in ochre. They were highly pleased when I said I was a Hindu monk belonging to their own religion. Now they wanted to know why I was going to Jain shrine for meditation. I replied: "I have regard for the prophets, saints, and sages of all religions. I have attended the Christian Mass and prayed in their churches. I have also meditated in the gurudwaras of Sikhs, and even in Muslim mosques, besides offering my worship at the temples belonging to all the various sects of Hinduism. But I prefer Jain shrines for their attractive setting, artistic and pleasing appearance, overall cleanliness, and the serene atmosphere prevailing in them."

The other thing which intrigued the villagers was my being allowed to stay at Samavasaran, where non-Jains were not allowed. I counter-questioned them: "Will a digambara Jain be allowed to stay at a svetambara dharmashala?" The reply came: "There was a time when they were not allowed, when a svetambara was also not allowed to stay in a digambara dharmashala." "Isn't it wrong?", I asked. "Do they not worship the same Lord Mahavira? Although a Hindu monk, I practice the same principles of truth, non-violence, continence, non-stealing, and non-covetousness which were preached by Lord Mahavira and are being practiced by the Jain Monks." Reciting from the *Siva-Mahimnah-Stotra*, I went on: "'*All these are various paths leading to the same goal, like so many rivers reaching the same ocean through various routes, straight or crooked.*' Why should a non-Jain not be allowed to stay in a Jain Dharmashala if he observes the rules and regulations and is not hostile to the Jaina faith and its basic tenets?"

Our conversation ended here and I went my way. I did not realize then that my stay at the Samavasaran Dharmashala had been made possible by a special permission obtained by R.S. from its manager on the assurance that all their rules would be observed. Jains do not allow their Dharmashalas, especially those attached to temples, to be converted into public hotels devoid of rules and religious sanctity. This is the reason why non-Jain tourists face the problem of lodging and board in spite of there being so many Dharmashalas.

After this talk, I ceased to be an object of curiosity, although children continued to remain at a safe distance from me. I saw some parents teaching their children to say "pranam" to me with folded hands. One lady, to quiet her weeping child, would often tell me, "Sadhu Baba, take away this child with you." I would smile and move on. One of the villagers who lived by the side of the road would meet me and talk to me often. I discussed with him the problem of village development. He was surprised, for he never expected a monk to talk of secular things. He frankly told me that until then he had thought that monks spent their time only in contemplation of God. He did not know anything of the Ramakrishna Mission and wanted to know more about it.

Ritualistic Worship

I was allowed to stay at the Jal Mandir for as long as I wished. Most pilgrims would have their darshan, do puja, sing devotional songs, and leave within a few minutes. At times a crowd of tourists would arrive, making the place noisy, but the moment they left, peace would return. Generally on Sundays there would be a greater rush, and the limited space within the shrine would be so crowded that I would be compelled to stay out all the time. I was amazed to see not only tourists, but devotees from all parts of India.

Being a revolt against Brahminism and Hindu ritualism, Jainism has wholly and successfully got rid of priestcraft. I noticed priests wearing the sacred thread at various temples, and on enquiry learnt that they were Hindu brahmins employed by the Jains to perform the daily worship and to assist Jain devotees to do worship. I noticed that they were treated also as paid servants by the Jains. A certain sect of Svetambar Jains does not worship images. Hence, its members neither go to temples nor do ritualistic worship. Instead, they offer their worship to the acharya or head of the Order. However, ritualism in a simplified form has entered into Jainism. There are books available in which procedures for various types of worship are described.

To pay my respects to Lord Mahavira, and to get acquainted with Jain rituals, I did one puja and evening arati at the Jal Mandir. Apart from bathing and putting on a washed dhoti and a chuddar to cover the upper part of the body, I had to tie a cloth on my face to cover the nose and mouth. Jain men, in their white, cream, or yellow silk puja dress, look very devout. First of all, the flowers and sandal paste sticking on the image were removed by washing with water and rubbing, if necessary, with a brush made by tying together khus straws. Now the image was bathed, first with milk and then with water, with the priest chanting the appropriate mantras. After this the image was thoroughly dried with the help of five pieces of fine cloth, one after the other. The procedure up to this is called praksalan or praksal. Now began the actual worship, which consisted of waving incense, applying sandal paste, offering flowers, and waving the lighted lamp. There were no preliminaries like nyasa, bhutasuddhi etc., as in Hindu puja. The articles of worship were purified simply by waving them once or twice over the lighted incense stick. Sandal paste was applied on the big toes, knees, forearms, shoulders, crown of head, forehead, neck, chest, navel, and palms, in that order. For each application there was a mantra. Time permitting, the image may be decorated with more sandal paste and flowers. A bell or a meal gong was rung while waving the lighted lamp. Evening arati consists of only waving the lamp, to the accompaniment of a hymn and ringing the bell, and lasts only four or five minutes. Digambara Jains do not offer sandal paste and flowers. Uncooked rice (aksata), dry sweets (naivedya) and fruits are also offered, although I did not offer them. The rice grains are arranged on the offering table to form a diagram consisting of a crescent on the top, three dots in the middle, and a swastika at the bottom. Over this diagram dry sweets like sugarcandy and lozenges are placed. There is no custom of taking prasada: whatever is offered goes to the Brahmin priest.

The mantras actually consist of couplets or poems in Gujarati or Hindi which the devotees can easily memorize. There are also a number of Pali texts which the devotees know by heart. Most women-devotees could sing the hymns, and did the puja themselves. It was interesting to see a lady in a group of devotees reciting long Pali texts fluently and guiding the rest like a priest, saying now and then: "Now chant navkar mantra four times," "now offer rice," etc. The mantra for making the final offering is in Sanskrit, beginning with Om and ending with Swaha. I also saw a group of South Indian Jains doing elaborate worship to each of the twenty-four tirthankaras with Sanskrit verses and with a number of bija mantras.

End of Pilgrimage

During my sojourn I once went to Rajgir and met the aged Jain saint, Sri Amar Muni. He said that like the twelve sacred Siva temples of Hinduism, famous for their jyotirlingas, Rajgir and Nalanda too are jyotirmaya, luminous with the light of spirituality. He advised me to meditate in the Jal Mandir at night when Pavapur becomes intensely calm. The saint's wish was fulfilled and, as the crowning event of my stay. I spent the last night at the Jal Mandir. As the night advanced, the calm started deepening, and by midnight even the shouts of the night guards and the barking of dogs were silenced. One felt as if one were in a realm beyond time and space.

Generally, aspirants are not able to derive spiritual benefit from shrines belonging to sects other than their own. If, however, they could attune themselves to the spiritual vibrations of the Jaina tirthankara which pervades Pavapuri, they could derive great benefit by doing spiritual practices there. But, as in most centers of pilgrimages, here, too, various kinds of disturbance occur, and these have to be borne with patience.

My memorable days at Pavapuri came to an end all too soon. As the car left Samavasaran and sped on the familiar serpentine road, I was aware of a change. The uniform greenish yellow carpet of rice fields which had earlier greeted me was no longer to be seen. In its place there stretched a gaunt landscape of bare brown earth, relieved occasionally by the dark green of the newly sprouted wheat, the bright yellow of mustard flowers, and the movements of tractors, bullocks, and ploughmen. The villagers had also changed. Those innocent eyes which had once stared at an unknown sannyasin with curiosity, were now wet with gratefulness for the now familiar monk of the Ramakrishna Order who had brought them the life-giving message of Sri Ramakrishna. Finally, I was conscious of a change within me too. There was a richness of experience, and a sense of fullness and peace which could be felt even after I returned to the din and bustle of city life.

A former editor of the Vedanta Keshari, Swami Brahmeshananda is a senior monk of the Ramakrishna Order and until recently was the Secretary of the Ramakrishna Mission Ashrama in Chandigarh, India. He is now retired and is living in Varanasi.

"The Song of the Free" by Swami Vivekananda

The wounded snake its hood unfurls,
The flame stirred up doth blaze,
The desert air resounds the calls
Of heart-struck lion's rage:

The cloud puts forth its deluge strength
When lightning cleaves its breast,
When the soul is stirred to its inmost depth
Great ones unfold their best!

Let eyes grow dim and heart grow faint
And friendship fail and love betray,
Let Fate its hundred horrors send
And clotted darkness block the way –

All nature wear one angry frown
To crush you out – still know, my soul,
You are Divine, March on and on,
Nor right nor left, but to the goal!

Nor angel I, nor man nor brute,
Nor body, mind, nor he nor she;
The books do stop in wonder mute
To tell my nature – I am He!

Before the sun, the moon, the earth,
Before the stars or comets free,
Before e'en Time has had its birth –
I was, I am, and I will be!

The beauteous earth, the glorious sun,
The calm sweet moon, the spangled sky,
Causation's laws do make them run,
They live in bonds, in bonds they die –

And mind its mantle, dreamy net,
Casts o'er them all and holds them fast,
In warp and woof of thought are set
Earth, hells, and heavens, or worst or best.

Know these are but the outer crust –
All space and time, all effect, cause,
I am beyond all sense, all thought,
The Witness of the Universe!

Not two nor many, 'tis but One.
And thus in me all me's I have,
I cannot hate, I cannot shun
Myself from me – I can but love!

From dreams awake, from bonds be free!
Be not afraid. This mystery,
My shadow, cannot frighten me!
Know once for all that I am He!

WISDOM FACETS FROM THE GEM OF TRUTH

Sri Ramakrishna

Holy Mother, Sri Sarada Devi

Make of Me the Same Brahman

"He who is called Brahman by the jnanis is known as Atman by the yogis and as Bhagavan by the bhaktas. The same Brahmin is called priest when worshiping in the temple, and cook when preparing a meal in the kitchen."

(Gospel of Sri Ramakrishna)

Of Radiant Hue

"One sees different colors through a prism; in reality, there is no such thing as color. Likewise, nothing exists, in reality, except Brahman. Brahman alone is real and the world is illusory. But there is an appearance of the manifold because of maya, egoism."

(Gospel of Sri Ramakrishna)

Vidya Shakti

"A wife endowed with spiritual wisdom is a real partner in life. She greatly helps her husband to follow the spiritual path. After the birth of one or two children they live like brother and sister. Both of them are devotees of God — His servant and His handmaid. Their family is a spiritual family. They are always happy with God and His devotees. They know that God alone is their own, from everlasting to everlasting. They are like the Pandava brothers; they do not forget God in happiness or in sorrow."

(Gospel of Sri Ramakrishna)

Adyashakti

"Brahman is actionless. When It is engaged in the processes of creation, preservation, and dissolution, It is called the Primal Power, Adyashakti. This power must be propitiated. It is so written in the Chandi. The gods first sang a hymn to the Adyashakti. Only then did Hari awake from His yogic sleep."

(Gospel of Sri Ramakrishna)

Unfair Exchange?

"Through the mantra, spiritual energy is transmitted — the guru's energy goes to the disciple, and the disciple's sins come over to the guru. That is why by imparting the mantra and taking over the sins, the body becomes afflicted with so many diseases. When the disciple commits a sin, the guru has to suffer for it along with him. That is why Rakhal does not want to give mantra. He says, 'Mother, I suffer from fever when I impart a mantra.' But we must remember, too, that the guru gets joy from the disciple's good qualities."

(The Compassionate Mother)

No such thing as a Motherless Child

"I am your true mother, a mother not by virtue of being your guru's wife, nor because of any assumed relationship, nor by way of empty talk. I am your true mother."

(Holy Mother, Sri Sarada Devi)

Three Great Statements

"Sri Ramakrishna left me behind to manifest the Motherhood of God. I have realization in the palm of my hand. Make no distinction between Sri Ramakrishna and me."

(The Mother as I Saw Her)

Please Practice Daily

"How can I sleep, my child? All my children come to me with great longing to take initiation, but most of them do not practice japa regularly. What to speak of regularly, they do nothing at all. And since I have accepted their responsibility, should I not see to their welfare? I do japa for their sake."

(Sri Sarada Devi, The Great Wonder)

Ma, Ma, Ma!

"If you cannot choose a name for japa, simply repeat 'Ma.'"

(The Gospel of Holy Mother)

WISDOM FACETS FROM THE GEM OF TRUTH

Swami Vivekananda   Sri Ramakrishna's Disciples & Devotees

Wear Out or Rust Out? — That is the Question

"To keep one's self steady in the midst of this whirl of kama-kanchana and hold on to one's own ideals until disciples are molded, and to conceive of the ideas of realization and perfect renunciation, is indeed difficult work. The body must go, no mistake about that. Why then let it go in idleness? 'It is better to wear out than rust out.'"

The Problem with this World....

"In this world, all things are done by people guided like lifeless machines. There is no mental activity, no unfoldment of the heart, no vibration of life, no flux of hope; there is no strong stimulation of the will, no experience of keen pleasure, nor the contact of intense sorrow; there is no stir of inventive genius, no desire for novelty, no appreciation of new things. Clouds never pass from this mind, the radiant picture of the morning sun never charms this heart. It never even occurs to the mind if there is any better state than this; where it does, it cannot convince; in the event of conviction, effort is lacking; and even where there is effort, lack of enthusiasm kills it out."

Give Up and Come To

"Those who want to help mankind must take their own pleasure and pain, name and fame, and all sorts of interests and make a bundle of them and throw them into the sea, and then come to the Lord. This is what all the Masters said and did. The fact is that the Lord is in us, we are He, the eternal subject, the real ego, never to be objectified, and that all this objectifying process is mere waste of time and talent. When the soul becomes aware of this it gives up objectifying and falls back more and more upon the subjective. This is the evolution, less and less in the body and more and more in the mind — man the highest form, meaning in Sanskrit, manas, thought — the animal that thinks, and not the animal that senses only." (All Selections, *Complete Works of Vivekananda*)

A God-Centered Life

"One day while meditating at home I had a vision of the omnipresent eyes of God. Those open eyes were all-pervading like the limitless sky. Thus every day in the morning and before going to sleep I would be absorbed in deep meditation and I would see the divine forms of various gods and goddesses. Then I would go to Dakshineswar and describe these visions to Sri Paramahamsadeva. Then I would massage his feet with his permission...."

(Swami Abhedananda, *My Life Story*)

"The Universe is Mind Made Manifest"

"Discussions and perusal of books containing dry arguments will only confuse your head. You must live in the company of holy men who have realized God or have made progress in that direction. But remember that everything depends mainly on your own mind. If your mind is not calm there is no use in your living for years in the most secluded place away from human habitations. You must sincerely pray to God to make your mind calm and to enable you to attain Him and when your mind wanders away you must try hard to bring it back...."

(*Mahapurush Maharaj as We Saw Him*)

Life-Saving Message

"Look here! Read the *Gospel of Sri Ramakrishna* every day. It contains Sri Ramakrishna's own words and is a very authentic document. Once Purna was in a very depressed state of mind, so much so that he decided to commit suicide. But he thought of first reading a little of the *Gospel of Sri Ramakrishna* before departing this world and decided that the words contained on the page that he opened first he would regard as the last words of Sri Ramakrishna to him. He opened and the page read, 'Sri Ramakrishna is thinking about Purna.' Everything changed. He thought, 'If the Master was thinking about him, why should he be depressed?'"

(*Monastic Disciples of Swami Vivekananda*)

SCRIPTURAL SAYINGS
of the World's Religious Traditions

"Feathered creatures like the swan fly through the air; fools who covet and possess psychic powers glide through the ethers. But the truly wise ones, having conquered desires and passions, go forth out of this world, never to return again to the realm of transmigration."

"The Atman, which is free of evil, free from old age, free from death, free of sorrow, free of hunger and thirst, whose desire is of the truth, whose resolve is of the truth — That should be sought; That, one should strive to comprehend.' For they who have found out and understood the Atman attain all worlds and all desires. Thus spoke Prajapati."

"Whoever wishes to attain to the highest perfection of his being and to the vision of the supreme good, must have a knowledge of himself as of the things about him to the very core. It is only so that he can arrive at the supreme clarity. Therefore learn to know thyself, for that is better for thee than to know all the powers of creation."

"Who is the wisest among men? Whosoever learns constantly from other men. Who is the richest among men? Whosoever is contented with his lot. Who is the strongest among men? Whosoever is most capable of self-mastery."

"Knowest thou not that thy life consists of only a few breaths? Why, then, hast thou lost thyself in the search for the mystery of life and death? Thou shalt rather seek out thy spiritual path before thy life is taken from thee. If living, ye find it not, then how can ye hope to find it after death?"

"A towering tree is at first a slender shoot; a nine-storied tower is raised by first placing a few small stones atop one another; a journey of a thousand leagues begins with a single step. Therefore, be careful of your thoughts, for they are the beginning of your acts."

Babaji Bob Kindler ◆

THE WONDER OF UNIVERSALITY

A Principle Whose Time has Come

Ephesians states that *"There is one body, and one Spirit."* If this is true, then ultimately there must be one religion as well. If we search deeply and specify it, we will find that its name is Universality, and its time is already upon us. In the Bhagavata Purana it is said that *"The idea of thou and I is a fruit of ignorance."* Oneness, then, solidarity on all levels of existence, represents our best and highest good. As Mohammed declared, peace be upon him: *"Seek the Truth, though you must go to China to find it."*

Superior to mere tolerance, far beyond eclecticism, even transcendent of a currently favored ecumenism, the principle of Universality is what the human race has been waiting and searching for, knowingly or unknowingly, over the entire span of its earthly existence. Up until recent times, culminating with the advent of Sri Ramakrishna Paramahamsa, this wide open, ultra-catholic vision had been conceived of, talked about, and acknowledged by sages and seers of the past, but none had ever brought it into the broad and open daylight of full maturation. The Great Master was born to do just that, and by taking up some of the main religions of the world, in addition to many of the major sects and lineages of Mother India, this incomparable soul practiced and championed them, without reserve or preference, to show that all of them led to the same essential goal.

It is important to note, when introducing such an expansive subject as Universality, that its main tenet is not one of comparison, or of superiority, but of all-inclusiveness. This is the intention of the Upanisads when they state that *"Goal is one, Paths are many."* Stated poetically and intrapersonally in those nondual scriptures, it means:

May we always and ever be,
like mighty rivers flowing into the sea,
merging all name, form, and identity,
into the ocean of Absolute Reality.

Further, the supreme doctrine of Universality does not declare that all religions are the same, but rather that they all give open way and access into the same essence. These, along with several other endearing facts, make the quest for the attainment of Universality one of great appeal and immediacy — an ideal whose time has come.

The Earmarkings of a Great Universalist

Universality is less of a practice and more of a position. Possessing this vast stance can be likened to mastering a superior mental and philosophical asana. With it in hand, and well comprehended, there is nothing the soul cannot see, no problem it cannot solve, no experience it cannot secure, and no limit it cannot breach. But its sweetest claim falls in the realm of true Religion where it allows for and facilitates the merging of many different streams of consciousness. In a telling admission from Sri Ramakrishna's own lips, related in an inspiring description of the consummation of His varied universal spiritual practices to His devotees, He said, *"I have gathered the fragrant flowers of many different religions of the world and fashioned a bouquet of them, offering it at the Fearless Feet of the Universal Wisdom-Mother."*

Not satisfied to offer a single flower of only one hue, a feat that even an exceptional religious man might find hard to achieve, the Great Master pierced through all barriers and entered the multi-faceted field of Universality itself, gaining access to the wisdom of all pathways there. It was an ingenious move all its own, and it stands today as an unprecedented occurrence and incomparable victory in the history of religion.

Many of the abundant gifts of this unique victory are to be felt and seen in the personage of Swami Vivekananda, often called the chief disciple of Sri Ramakrishna Paramahamsa. The great Swami was on fire with this singular vision during all of the brief 39 years of his life on this earth, wherein he took it upon himself to introduce the galvanizing subject of Universality to those who were ready for it. To read some of his own words on this superlative subject is to be immediately infected with the intensity of this fire, and to discover the tenets and characteristics of its boundless and eternal philosophy:

"Mankind ought to be taught that religions are but the varied expressions of The Religion which is Oneness, so that each may choose the path that suits him best. We believe that every being is divine, is God. Every soul is a sun covered over with clouds of ignorance; the difference between soul and soul is due to the difference in density of these layers of clouds. We believe that this is the conscious or unconscious basis of all religions, and that this is the explanation of the whole history of human progress either in the material, intellectual, or spiritual plane — the same Spirit is manifesting through different planes. We believe that this is the very essence of the Vedas. We believe that it is the duty of every soul to treat, think of, and behave as such, i.e., as Gods, and not hate or despair, or vilify, or try to injure them by any manner or means. This is the duty not only of the sannyasin, but of all men and women."

WAVES IN THE OCEAN OF MATURE UNIVERSALISM

"I have practiced the disciplines of all paths, each for a few days. Otherwise I would have had no peace of mind. I respect the Shaktas, the Vaishnavas, the Vedantists, and also the modern Brahmajnanis. Therefore, people of all sects come to me. And everyone of them think that I belong to his school." — Sri Ramakrishna

Universalism

universalism / n: a principle corresponding to reality and its essence which declares that all beings will be saved based upon a truth that is comprehensively broad and versatile, existent and operative everywhere and under all conditions, that embraces the totality of mankind without limits or exceptions regardless of religious differences, and that is easily adaptable or adjustable to meet the varied philosophical requirements of all of humanity.

Ecumenism

ecumenism / n: of or relating to an entire body of churches, particularly of one religious tradition.

Eclecticism

eclecticism / n: to select what appears to be best from a number of various doctrines or methods.

"I have gathered the many different religions of the world and fashioned a bouquet of them, offering it at the Fearless Feet of the Universal Wisdom-Mother." — Ramakrishna

Fundamentalism

fundamentalism / n: a movement of 20th century Protestantism stressing the literal interpretation of the Bible as the only truth.

"We reject none, neither theist, pantheist, monist, polytheist, agnostic, nor atheist; the only condition of being a disciple is modeling a character at once the broadest and most intense. We leave everybody free to know, select, and follow whatever suits and helps him." — Swami Vivekananda

Atheism

atheism / n: the doctrine which proposes a basic disbelief in the existence of God or deity.

Agnosticism

agnosticism / n: the doctrine which espouses the belief that God is unknown and unknowable.

Intellectualism

intellectualism / n: devotion to the exercise of the intellect and to rational intellectual pursuits.

"Dry knowledge is like cheap fireworks, or a rocket that bursts into a few sparks and dies away. But spiritual knowledge is like an expensive rocket that showers different colors, stops, then bursts forth again many times. Yet, the minds of pundits and scholars are fixed on dry knowledge, like the eyes of a vulture fixed on the carrion pit." — Ramakrishna

Secularism

secularism / n: indifference to or rejection or exclusion of religion and religious considerations.

Materialism

materialism / n: preoccupation with matter to the exclusion of intellectual and spiritual considerations based upon the belief that matter is the only reality.

"There once was a man who owned a dye-tub. Such was its wonderful property that people could dye their clothes any color they desired by merely dipping them into it. Observing this unusual phenomena, one clever man approached the owner of the tub and said, 'Sir, please dye my cloth the color of the dye in your tub.'" — Sri Ramakrishna

Chart by Babaji Bob Kindler   Property of SRV Associations

Defining Terms

A complete definition of the very word "Universality," even if wrought from the pages of an English dictionary, is extremely telling. No doubt that men, even of a secular turn of mind, being desirous of peace on earth, have contemplated the possibility of Universality in the past, even when lacking a name for it. Such ponderings gave rise to idealistic definitions, nonetheless. The paragraph which follows has been laced together from four different definitions drawn from Webster's Dictionary around the word Universalism.

universalism / n: a principle corresponding to reality and its essence which declares that all beings will be saved based upon a truth that is comprehensively broad and versatile, existent and operative everywhere and under all conditions, that embraces the totality of mankind without limits or exceptions regardless of religious differences, and that is easily adaptable or adjustable to meet the varied philosophical requirements of all of humanity.

It is easy to feel the high-mindedness and the underlying enthusiasm in this pregnant sentence, even given the usual sterility of the dictionary format. Who would not lend an immediate ear and snap to attention when such lofty ideas are rendered into words? Further, and of note, the absence of narrow-mindedness and bigotry is the first thing to catch the mind's eye here, all enhanced by the appealing phrase, "regardless of religious differences."

Universalism in Action

But far beyond even inspiration, Swami Vivekananda proposed placing such exhilarating ideas and their vibrations into action for the highest good of all beings, and did so while simultaneously proposing solutions for the seemingly insurmountable problems involved. Writing in his letters, he stated the ideal with lucidity: *"We want to lead humanity to the place where there is neither the Vedas, the Bible, or the Koran; yet this has to be done by harmonizing the Vedas, Bible, and Koran. Let some of you spread like wildfire, then, and preach the worship of the universal aspect of God — a thing that has never been undertaken before in our country. No quarreling with people; we must be friends with all."*

Whereas the idea, or truism, of one God, one Reality, is not at all unknown or uncommon to the varied religious traditions of the world, the problem is that the followers of these main world movements all practice the *"my watch keeps the only right time"* theory, as Sri Ramakrishna observed in His lifetime. But He followed up this statement with a plea that all beings check their religious and philosophical watches with the sun to get correct time. The sundial is the illumined soul, and the sun is the experience of nonduality — a mainstay in the principle of Universality. These two, when approached, will render the exact time to striving beings, thus relieving them of narrowness and hypocrisy. Under the discriminating and all-revealing sunlight of Universality, all religions are seen to be guilty of such errors — Hinduism included.

But Mother India is much more than conventional Hinduism, just as Christ is far more than Christianity could ever reveal. India does not base its many-sided view of Truth on just one holy book and one prophet, but has seen dozens and hundreds over a vast sweep of time. Each one of these views (darshanas) and beings (rishis) became a window into Reality, having blazed a path inwardly to Truth. Their unanimous concurrence over long sweeps of time on matters of the Spirit lent even more weight to the apt conclusions that were drawn from direct experience along the pathway to Enlightenment.

Universality in ancient Bharata was both present as an underlying tenet and being forged as an ideal for humanity over the many millennia that the Indian seer focused upon spirituality. It was only natural, then, that it needed a testing ground upon which to announce its gifts and its supremacy as an ideal for mankind. At the Parliament of Religions, held in Chicago in 1893, Swami Vivekananda brought the twin aspects of Nondualism (advaita) and Universality (Sanatana Dharma) to the West under the title of Vedanta, introducing western man to the wonders of true religion, living philosophy, and authentic spirituality. About that occurrence he later wrote: *"The Parliament of Religions was organized with the intention of proving the superiority of the Christian Religion over other forms of faith, but the philosophic religion of Hinduism was able to maintain its position notwithstanding."*

Far more than merely maintaining their positions, Vedanta, Buddhism, Taoism, and other "foreign" religions not only gained a foothold in America and England, but gained a growing following as well. It was not long before monks and lay persons from other lands reached western shores and began the work of transmitting to its people the tenets of living a truly spiritual life in the world which, after all, is the real acid test for the authenticity of religion and philosophy. In this regard, the great Swami advised that his students and disciples of Vedanta live an active spiritual life, telling them: *"However sublime be the theories, however well-spun may be the philosophy, I do not call it religion so long as it is confined to books and dogmas."* Therefore, the first real obstacles for the advent of Universality — lack of exposure and misunderstanding — were encountered and removed by this modern day spiritual Hercules. The result has been, that for the past one hundred and twenty years (1893-2013), actual spirituality (not just conventional followings or diluted religion mixed with politics) has achieved a foothold in the West, with the presence of Advaita Vedanta, with the advent of Buddhism, in forms of Zen, Tibetan Buddhism, and other flourishing traditions.

Worldliness — A Chronic Disease

Besides the resistance of fundamentalist religion and its shortsighted followers, there exists in the West the considerable impediment of a combined apathy mixed with a tenacious ignorance around the true Self of mankind. In the West, those who profess religion still believe in such untenable assumptions as an eternal hell fire, heaven as an ultimate goal, and the sinful nature of mankind. In Swami Vivekananda's time, they had, and still have to a great degree, no idea about the birthless, deathless essence of Reality, the nontransformational nature of Existence, and the unoriginated status of the Soul and Nature. To say the least, without the recognition of the divine nature of mankind in acknowledgement, Universality and its companion principles will not be able to make a lasting impression upon embodied beings, what to speak of revealing to them the nondual Truth and destroying thereby their sufferings for all time.

It was thus that Swami Vivekananda, in both the West and his own country, undertook to introduce his "man making" regimen to all, and to return human beings back to true Religion so as to recover their divine birthright. He advised, *"Work hard, be steady, and have faith in the Lord. Keep the motto before you, 'Elevation of the masses without injuring religion.' Can you raise the masses? Can you give them back their lost individuality without making them lose their innate spirituality?"*

Thus, with the mold struck and the task uncovered, Vivekananda went forth to establish a firm and solid religious and philosophical ground upon which an initial semblance of the truth of Universality could be set. As he did this, he utilized the past experiences of his own country to post as warnings for the workers for the desired Universality of the present. Speaking about the uneducated and impatient reformer, and the fire-darting religious zealot, he noted: *"The modern reformers saw no way to reform but by first crushing out the religion of India. They tried and they failed. Why? Because few of them ever studied their own religion, and not one ever underwent the training necessary to understand the Mother of all Religions."*

What a novel idea, to actually practice the religion of one's birth, of one's choice! And far more importantly, that those who move to make changes in society do so, for to understand any society one would need to comprehend the moving force which underlies it — mainly, God. Further, and as Vivekananda's pointed statement above reflects, an intellectual study of religion will not be enough. Training will necessary. A money and profit-centered priest class occupying a religious institution that is disconnected from both the truths of religion and the needs of spiritual aspirants cannot provide such training. Seers, sages, saints, and other luminaries will need to be on hand, for these have renounced worldly undertakings and have little to do with money, fame, power, and other potentially corrupting influences.

And so, Swami Vivekananda pointed out the importance of both understanding and practicing the religion of one's choice before engaging in its manifestations and expressions. To him, cosmology, philosophy, religion, and growing spirituality were to be ground to perfection in the crucible of practice in order that the finest of all admixtures could be applied like a healing salve to mankind's problems in relativity.

Universality's Undying, Underlying Tenets

For those who had already possessed religion through any of its different pathways, Swami Vivekananda moved to inform them of the nondual thread which wove all of them together like a string of precious pearls. This oft-spoken but seldomly realized oneness, he taught, applied to both Religion and to the human soul as well. Without the knowledge of both, existing in union and perfection, Universality would have little chance of working its way into the modern mind of mankind, what to speak of winning over the human heart. About the crucial import of this, he wrote: *"The soul has neither sex, nor caste, nor imperfection. We believe that nowhere in the Vedas, Darshanas, or Puranas, or Tantras, it is ever said that the soul has any sex, creed or caste. Dualist, qualified monist, monist, shaiva, vaishnava, shakta, even the Buddhist and the Jain and others — whatever sects have arisen in India are all at one in this respect: that infinite power is latent in this jivatman (individualized soul); from the ant to the perfect man there is the same Atman in all, the difference being only in manifestation."*

If a very deep inspection of the revealed scriptures of India — Upanisads, Bhagavad Gita, Brahma Sutras, Ashtavakra Samhita, Avadhuta Gita, Adhyatma Ramayana — is engaged in, the like of which Swami Vivekananda undertook during his lifetime, two veritable axioms are noticed above all else. These two have both fortified India's Religion and kept it from dying out over the "long efflux of time." Tellingly, these two are all but missing (or distorted beyond recognition or heavily interpolated out of existence) in western religious texts and movements, yet they form the very crux of nonduality which is like "wind to a bird's wings, or a breath of air to a drowning man." The long-range existence and longevity of a principle like Universality depends on axioms like these two, which sported direct and exacting words and terminology in Indian philosophy from time immemorial.

Referring imminently to the Soul, Atman, *Aparinama* (changelessness, immutability, nontransformation), and *Ajativada* (birthlessness, deathlessness, eternity, immortality), best reflect Truth as it is known and seen in all the Indian darshanas. Comprehension of these two maxims of Existence, achieved after rapt contemplation, concentration, and meditation, frees the apparently transmigrating soul (mental complex) from all of its doubts and limitations. The soul's sufferings will go too, for they are caused by the mind's failings and meanderings, its delusions and incertitudes around the nature of Reality. How does this transformation work?

When the mind reaches assurance via direct spiritual experience based upon spiritual practice (sadhana), that both God (Brahman) and the Soul (Atman) are identical, and remain the same despite external changes, then it experiences Peace. Further, when, inside of this Great Peace, all changing things — elements, nature, objects, beings — are perceived as apparently changing only and, further still, are seen as thought projections of one's own mind, then a supreme and detached Witness Consciousness comes to the fore wherein all movement, internal and external, is known to be nonactual.

All of this is the gift of cognizing Aparinama, nontransformation. In other words, transformation of any kind is not possible in Reality due to its eternally stable and homogenous nature. Words such as "homogenous," or "all-pervasive," are the only words in the English language that are effective for explaining these subtlest of nuances. To use Lord Krishna's words from the *Bhagavad Gita*, and speaking from the personal standpoint first, He states: *"Beings of poor understanding think of Me, the Unmanifest, as having manifestation, not knowing my Supreme State — immutable and unsurpassed. This deluded world knows Me not, the Unborn, the Unchanging."* Then speaking transpersonally, He declares: *"There is a higher Awareness that changes not, even when all other things seem to change. Reaching realization of That, there is*

> "We have given war a chance; peace also got its turn. Neither have worked. What is needed is "uni," "verse," "al," "iti" — this one refrain affirmed by all beings. It is why great beings come to earth, and why they return again and again — to see if we have finally understood and successfully implemented it into the life of the planet."

no more change, no more coming and going, no more movement of any kind."

This statement ushers in the second principle connected to Universality, called Ajativada — the path of those who know no birth, no death. Its lofty boons apply to the embodied being's highest aspirations, and provide a soothing balm for its doubts, fears, and misgivings. This principle is what inspired great stotrams sung by profound nondualists like Shankara. In the fifth verse of his *Nirvana Shatakam*, he utters:

na mrityur na shanka   na me jati bhedha
pita naiva me naiva   mata na janma.

"Death nor fear I have none, nor any distinction of caste; Neither father nor mother, nor even a birth have I....."

Sri Krishna visits and revisits this theme of Ajativada in the sacred scripture, *Bhagavad Gita* again and again, for the elucidation and destruction of fear in his beloved disciple, Arjuna. Giving the young warrior two options, one of the highest Truth, the other of a practical bent, He states: *"You should know this one truth, Arjuna: the Soul, Atman, is unborn and free of death. It is never subject to transmigration and other changes. But if you cannot comprehend this yet, then think on this: Everything that is born, dies, and that which dies gets born again. Where is the grief in this?"*

At first, then, axioms like Ajativada are perplexing and hard to grasp, especially for the soul born and raised in cultures that think only in terms of birth and death, and base their existence on life of the body and deny life of the Soul. Yet, Eternal Life was a main theme of the Christ, representing a fundamental part of his teaching. In Swami Vivekananda's way of thinking, *"Material science can only give worldly prosperity, whilst spiritual science is for eternal life. If there be no eternal life, still the enjoyment of spiritual thoughts as ideals is keener and makes a man happier, whilst the foolery of materialism leads to competition and undue ambition and ultimate death, individual and national. Instead of materializing the Spirit, i.e., dragging the spiritual to the material plane, convert the matter into Spirit, and try to live in it day and night. Seek not, touch not with your toes even, anything that is uncanny. Let your souls ascend day and night like an unbroken string unto the feet of the Beloved whose throne is in your own hearts and let the rest take care of themselves, i.e., the body and all else. If there be glory in keeping the machine in good trim, it is more glorious to withhold the soul from suffering with the body — that is the only demonstration of your being 'not matter' by letting matter alone."*

Philosophically, then, the appeal of Universality is undeniable. For the lover of Truth, its presence and existence is inviolable, its reign, unimpeachable. It only remains for all beings to proclaim its advent here on earth with unanimous assent. We have given war a chance; peace also got its turn. Neither have worked. What is needed is "uni—verse—all—iti," this one refrain affirmed by all beings. It is what has been vouchsafed to mankind in the form of sublime teachings over many ages, century after century. It is why great seers and sages have come to earth, and why they return again and again — to see if we have finally understood and implemented it into the life of the planet. We should not disappoint them, and cease tormenting them with our incredulity. To close with Swamiji's words:

"Acceptance, love, toleration for everything sincere and honest — but never for hypocrisy — this is true universality. My Master used to say that these names, Hindu, Christian, etc., stand as great bars to all brotherly feelings between man and man. We must try to break them down first. They have lost all their good powers and now only stand as baneful influences under whose black magic even the best of us behave like demons. Let everything go on as it is, only take care that no form becomes necessary. Unity is variety, see that universality is not hampered in the least. Everything must be sacrificed, if necessary, for that one sentiment, universality. Whether I live or die, whether I go back to India or not, remember this specifically, that universality — perfect acceptance, not tolerance only — is what we preach and perform."

Babaji Bob Kindler is the spiritual director of the SRV Associations with centers in Hawaii, Oregon, and California. A teacher of religion and spirituality and a prolific author, his books include *The Avadhut, Twenty-Four Aspects of Mother Kali, Ten Divine Articles of Sri Durga, Sri Sarada Vijnanagita, Swami Vivekananda Vijnanagita, An Extensive Anthology of Sri Ramakrishna's Stories, A Quintessential Yoga Vasishtha,* and *Reclaiming Kundalini Yoga*. Founder and Artistic Director of Jai Ma Music, he is also an accomplished musician and composer who has produced over twenty-five albums of instrumental and devotional music to date.

◆ *Sheikh Nur Al-Jerrahi*

TAKING HAND IN SUFISM
Its Four Steps & Seven Levels

Taking Refuge, receiving the Sacred Thread, taking Mantra-diksha, being Baptized — with inspirations such as these the aspiring spiritual seeker makes a huge commitment to intensify the search for Enlightenment via the sacred religious tradition of his or her choice. In Sufism, the term of divine endearment is "Taking Hand," which, as in other traditions, places the acolyte directly in the presence of teacher, teachings, pathway, and Divine Reality Itself. This is *"authentic initiation into a Mystic Order."*

My central responsibility in our Dervish Order is to offer initiation and to interpret dreams, which indicate Divine Permission to receive initiation and to advance along the mystic path, characterized by Nureddin Jerrahi by means of twenty-eight Divine Names. Among the four hundred major branches of the Dervish Orders, the path is most often characterized by eight Divine Names, sometimes by twelve, rarely by eighteen. That Pir Nureddin selected twenty-eight indicates that he placed the Divine Seal upon the fullness of the mystic way of Islam.

In the Jerrahi Order, one central initiation offers all the blessings of the path, rather than a series of successive initiations that certain other Orders prescribe. This initiation ceremony is not secret. It is often performed in the presence of visitors to the tekke, the dervish meeting hall. I have conducted this rite of entrance and sacrament of spiritual completeness for more than five hundred sincere aspirants, so it has become natural to me, almost like breathing. This ceremony always remains a moving experience for the community as a whole, for myself, for the initiate, and for the mature brothers or sisters who stand on each side of the new *dervish*, linking arms and helping the aspirant take these four ultimate steps.

The initiation is called "taking hand." It sacramentally replicates the historical event in the life of the Prophet when certain companions, already loyal to the holy way of life, ceremonially clasped his right hand, marking a vast intensification of their commitment. This act of taking hand creates a unique bond with the beloved Muhammad, beyond the respect and loyalty devout Muslims feel for their noble Prophet, upon him be peace. The right hand that is offered and received in this reenactment, therefore, is ultimately the right hand of the Prophet. The right hand of the *shaykh* is simply a conduit. Out of traditional Islamic courtesy, women initiates do not usually clasp the hand of the shaykh but both hold the same set of prayer beads.

The ceremony is a mystic crowning in which the Crown of Light, usually given to the soul in Paradise, is actually conferred here on earth. Those gifted by Allah with spiritual sight can perceive light, or even a crown of light, descending over the head of the new dervish at the appropriate moment. The Crown of Paradise can be transmitted only in Paradise; therefore Paradise consciousness must become fully present during the initiation. The invisible crown is usually symbolized by the gift of a white cap to the men and a white or colored veil to the women, although many modern women prefer the cap.

Receiving this crown enables one to experience Paradise consciousness here and now, during one's prayers and even during the struggles of daily life. The initiated dervishes can now transmit at least a glimpse of Paradise to their loved ones and colleagues, not verbally but directly, thereby elevating all humankind. The dervishes are not seeking their own spiritual bliss, but are clearly motivated by the longing to be of service to humanity, and to their own society in particular.

The First Step, First Pillar

The Shaykh gestures to the experienced dervishes to help the initiate make the first step, beginning with the right foot. The Islamic greetings of peace — *as-salam alaykum, alaykum assalam* — are exchanged, and the Shaykh welcomes the initiate to the dimension of *sharia*, the depth of the Sacred Law. I welcome aspirants to this exalted level by reminding them that sharia is essentially the repetition of the affirmation of Unity, *la ilaha illallah*, externally or internally, verbally or nonverbally, with every breath, every step, every intention, every perception. From this primary pillar of Islam, the other four pillars extend. I remind the aspirant that sharia is the way of constant prayerfulness and delight in the prayers, the way of ceaseless acts of generosity and kindness to all beings as one family of consciousness, and the way of fasting — not just abstaining from food and drink from dawn to sunset during *Ramadan*, but fasting at all times, waking and sleeping, from limited conceptuality and limited emotionality. Finally, sharia is the way of holy pilgrimage, but not just to the earthly *Kaaba* in the noble city of Mecca. Sharia is to remain constantly in the open and submitted state of a pilgrim while approaching the true Kaaba, the secret heart of humanity, where the diamond of Divine Essence is concealed from the conventional gaze of the world. This first step, the noble sharia, is obviously not just for beginners, nor is it left behind by the next three steps.

Step Two

The Shaykh beckons the dervish to take another step, and the process is repeated as the aspirant is welcomed to the *tariqa*.

This is the steeply ascending path the Holy *Quran* speaks about, the upward spiraling path that traverses the seven levels of consciousness. This is the path of profound purification, the path of mystic dreams and their inspired interpretation, the path of the joyful uproar and sweet companionship of the dervish lovers of Truth. The tariqa is a mystic tree — its spreading roots the beloved Prophet Muhammad, its noble trunk the sublime *Ali*. The great branches of this tree of Tariqa are the *Pirs* who have founded initiatory lineages, and the smaller limbs are all the noble *shaykhs* and *shaykhas*. The flowers of all colors and fragrances that grow from these branches are the countless dervishes. The fruits are love and wisdom. The sap of this tree is the ecstasy of conscious union with Reality.

The Welcome of the Third Step

The Shaykh gestures again and welcomes the aspirant to the third step, the *haqiqa*, the peak of the mountain of light. Here the path disappears into the boundless green meadow of Truth. Here in Truth alone, the aspirant and the entire community are asked to gaze with the eyes of the heart. Now one can perceive only a shoreless ocean of light — indescribable and inconceivable, without any division or partition, without surface or depth. This ocean of Divine Light is not placid but always filled with giant waves of love. The aspirant is now asked to focus on the eyes of the heart themselves, perceiving that they, too, are composed purely of Divine Light. This is the mystery of *nurun ala nur*, the Light of *Allah* within the Light of Allah.

The Final Step

The Shaykh beckons a fourth time, and the new dervish takes the final step onto the white sheepskin, laid out in front of the kneeling guide to symbolize the sacrifice of the ego. This is the *marifa*, the courageous descent of the dervish soul from the peak of light into the valley of suffering, struggle, sacrifice, and responsibility, while retaining the conscious union with Truth characteristic of the third step. The culmination of wisdom is to become dust beneath the feet of humanity. Marifa is the selfless service of humankind and of creation as a whole, demonstrated by the beloved Jesus, upon him be peace, when he washed the feet of his disciples at the Last Supper, thereby opening their hearts and illumining their minds. The hands of the new dervish now become the Divine Energies, *rahman* and *rahim*, Compassion and Mercy. The heart of the dervish becomes Divine justice and Divine Love. The breath of the dervish becomes Divine Life. The eyes of the dervish perceive only Divine Beauty. The mind of the dervish operates only with Divine Clarity and by the principle of Divine Unity.

The special protector and guide for sharia is the beloved Moses, for tariqa the beloved Jesus, for haqiqa the beloved Abraham, and for marifa the Seal of Messengers, the Distributor of the Light of Prophecy to all Hearts, the beloved Muhammad Mustafa, upon him be peace. A distinct spiritual energy is experienced at each of the four steps. The harmony of all four is ineffably beautiful.

Now the initiate kneels knee-to-knee with the Shaykh, firmly clasping his right hand or prayer beads. The Shaykh prays that the inconceivable Divine Mercy, which is always descending as an invisible rain upon the planetary plane and upon the human heart, should now become visible to the eyes of the heart, cleansing the entire being of the initiate from all misunderstandings or partial understandings imposed since childhood by the limited society or arising from the narrow structures of the limited self. The Shaykh prays that even the slightest shadow of the negation of love should be swept away from this aspiring heart and that it should be filled entirely with Divine Light. Together, the new dervish and the attending senior dervishes, along with the Shaykh and the entire community, repeat eleven times the Arabic phrase *estaghfirullah*, which opens the mind entirely to the power of Divine Forgiveness.

Whenever the Shaykh welcomes a new dervish to the four steps or prays for the aspirant, his words become Divine Energy and bring directly into being, before the eyes of the heart, precisely what is described or prayed, not as an abstraction or as a pious wish but as living Reality. This is the mystery of Divine Creativity described by the Holy Quran. Allah Most High simply calls out the Word of Power, Be! and whatever He wills directly and effortlessly comes into being.

At this point in the ancient ceremony of taking hand, the Quranic passage describing the original event in the desert of Arabia is melodiously chanted. I interpret the Divine Words to the new dervish in this way. When the lovers of Love linked the righthand side of their being with the Prophet of Love, upon him be peace, the mystic right hand of Divine Presence descended upon that linking. In this way Allah confirms the original promise made to the noble Adam. This promise has been passed in an unbroken stream of light through 124,000 Prophets to the beloved Muhammad of Arabia and transmitted from him through fourteen centuries of mystic shaykhs. This is the promise of the soul's union with its Lord in the bridal chamber of Divine Love, the promise that even the veils of soul and Lord will vanish in the supreme realization of identity. Naming the place and year before the eyes of these honorable witnesses, I add that here and now this Divine Promise, which is good until the End of Time, is again being confirmed.

Divine Affirmation at Seven Levels

Now the affirmation of Unity, la ilaha illallah, is repeated together by Shaykh and aspirant seven times, once for each level of consciousness, the seventh repetition occurring at the level where only Divine Consciousness exists. The Shaykh concludes the seventh affirmation by intoning *muhammad rasulallah*, Muhammad is the Messenger of Allah, and the dervish community begins to sing, in a beautiful traditional melody, the call of Divine Transcendence, *allahu akbar*, the affirmation of Unity and praises of the Prophet. The Shaykh now confers the cap or veil, greeting it thrice with a noble kiss, touching it to eyes and forehead, then offering it to the new dervish to greet in the same manner. The Shaykh places the traditional prayer beads of Islam into the right hand of the fully initiated brother or sister, symbolizing that every breath has now become equivalent to repeating one of the Divine Names. The astonishing fact of initiation is that the dervish has been transformed, before our eyes, into a person of perpetual prayer. His or her individual existence has now become ceaseless Divine Remembrance.

Spontaneous Prayer of the Shaykh

The Shaykh opens his palms and allows words of prayer to stream spontaneously through his heart to his lips. Whatever is appropriate for the initiate is now prayed in a graceful and uplifting manner, precisely as Allah has foreordained. I often conclude this long prayer by supplicating Allah Most High that our Pir Nureddin Jerrahi fix his spiritual gaze upon the heart of the new dervish, night and day, filling it with the Light of Universal Islam, that his saintly mother Amina Taslima transmit her purity and sanctity to this dervish, and that the representative of Pir Nureddin to modern humanity, Muzaffer Ashqi, fill the heart of this dervish with the exquisite wine of Love.

The newly invested dervish kisses the hand of the Shaykh, exactly as if kissing the hand of Pir and of Prophet, stands, and makes the same four steps backward, beginning with the left foot, which symbolizes the mystic way as the right foot symbolizes the sacred law. The atmosphere has now become light, joyous, playful. I reassure the new brother or sister that these four steps backward are not retreat or regression, that none of the spiritual riches of the four steps can be lost, but that one is simply returning to the existential situation, to realize and actualize these sublime gifts that now remain radiant at the core of his or her being. We do not enter the path to engage in religious fantasy, but to become more realistic, more free from self-deception, more uncompromising about Truth.

> "....none of the spiritual riches of the four steps can be lost....one is simply returning to the existential situation, to realize and actualize these sublime gifts that now remain radiant at the core of his or her being. We do not enter the path to engage in religious fantasy, but to become more realistic, more free from self-deception, more uncompromising about Truth."

I now request the entire community to embrace the new dervish or dervishes, for often friends or family members take the four steps together, arms linked in mutual, loving support, hearts merged in the beautiful state of eternal companionship. In traditional Muslim circles, the sisters embrace the sisters and the brothers embrace the brothers, but among North American and Mexican dervishes, these culturally ingrained restrictions often cannot be imposed. After all, the dervishes are one family. There are tears and laughter. The Divine Light shining from the countenance of the newly unveiled dervish is an undeniable, empirical fact.

Sacred Dream Interpretation

The most intimate teaching in our Dervish Order comes through spiritual dreams and their inspired interpretation. The shaykh does not deal with psychological or merely stress-releasing dreams, nor is there any fixed system of dream symbolism. Two dervishes came to our previous Grand Shaykh and reported the same dream: climbing a minaret and giving the Call to Prayer. To the first, the inspired interpreter commented, "You are going on pilgrimage. Make preparations." To the second, he remarked, "You have taken something that does not belong to you. Discover what that is and give it back." Before taking hand the aspirant often receives a significant dream of Divine Permission or, in some cases, Divine Insistence. After taking hand one usually experiences a dream confirming that the ceremony was accepted by Allah. In the context of Islamic spirituality, no sacred rite is considered to be automatically effective. Rather, one must seek and await signs of the Good Pleasure of Allah Most High.

Seven Levels of Consciousness

One of the fundamental teachings, shared by the various intertwining lineages of initiation that form the tree of Tariqa, concerns the seven levels of consciousness. Upon this crystal clear analysis of evolutionary levels, the esoteric teachings of Sufism are firmly based.

One does not have to consult ancient textbooks to discover the perennial teaching of Sufism. This esoteric map of consciousness was transmitted with accuracy and clarity in a spiritual dream granted by Allah through the blessings of Pir Nureddin Jerrahi to a Mexican girl of twelve. Along with her mother, father, and younger brother, Rahima had participated in the ceremony of taking hand about a year before her extraordinary dream. While visiting Mesquita Maria de la Luz, the Mosque of the Mother of the Prophet in Mexico City, where our Order is led by a gifted and dedicated woman, Amina Taslima al-Jerrahi, I was honored to hear and interpret this dream. In my role as guide, I have listened to thousands of profound dreams during the last eleven years. This one is among the most astonishing. A young girl, with the simple, natural imagery appropriate to her own psyche, accurately pictured the most sophisticated esoteric teaching of Islamic mysticism.

As I listened to her father, Abdul Qadir, translate his daughter's dream from Spanish to English, I began to realize what an immense gift this was to our Order, for we hold in common the spiritual wealth of our dreams and their interpretations. The powerful blessing of a mystic dream does not belong exclusively to the individual dreamer. Its healing, integration, and illumination belong to the entire community. I believe that Rahima's blessed dream of the seven levels of consciousness belongs as well to the lovers of Truth across the whole planet into the distant future.

Rahima dreamed that she was guided by someone she did

> "Two dervishes came to our previous Grand Shaykh and reported the same dream: climbing a minaret and giving the Call to Prayer. To the first, the inspired interpreter commented, 'You are going on pilgrimage. Make preparations.' To the second, he remarked, 'You have taken something that does not belong to you. Discover what that is and give it back.'

not recognize through a large house with seven floors. The ground floor was dirt. There were absolutely no signs of human habitation or refinement. The place was not even kept clean. The second floor was an extremely simple dwelling — bare wooden floor, bed, chair, table. It was kept clean and was attractive in its modest way. The third floor was a very comfortable home, according to modern standards. There were carpets, radio, television, refrigerator, and so forth.

When Rahima was taken to the fourth floor, the fourth level of consciousness, she was amazed to find a brilliant palace — marble floors, high ceilings, large gilded mirrors, beautiful antique furniture, precious ancient vases, and other works of art. At this point in the recounting of the dream, I began to realize that certain mysteries of the spiritual path, which remained vague to me, were about to be displayed in simple, dramatic imagery. All who were present entered a mild state of ecstasy, a gift of the fourth level. Rahima continued speaking, calmly and confidently, without any self-consciousness.

When the dreamer was guided to the fifth floor, she encountered total darkness, filled with a deep, rumbling music that she, as a twelve-year-old, found rather unsettling. When taken to the sixth floor, she found an empty, candle-lit space where a circle of dervishes, wearing white and kneeling on sheepskins, were engaged in the ancient ceremony of Divine Remembrance.

Arriving at the seventh floor, Rahima entered a brilliant, sunlit room, illuminated through large skylights and filled with lush green plants. No person was present, nor were there indications of human habitation. The golden light and the dark green of the leaves created a joyful, expansive feeling. Suddenly, one of the plants reached toward her with a long creeper, wrapped around her waist, and gently threw her out an open window. She fell with equal gentleness to the earth below, landing on her feet.

Almost as an afterthought, Rahima mentioned that her guide took her back through the same sevenfold structure several times, so that she was perfectly clear about the various levels. Each time, she was thrown out the window again. I asked her how many times she ascended these floors. She thought carefully for a moment, then replied, definitively, "Four times."

Shaykh Nur's Interpretation of the Seven Levels of Existence

The interpretation of this dream can be extensive. I offered a seminar in Mexico City on the seven levels of consciousness, during which I spoke about this dream for several hours.

The first level is the domineering self, basis for the aggressiveness, territoriality, and violent urge for survival that seriously threaten the coherence of our personhood, our society, and our planet. There is nothing intrinsically human here. There is no possibility for hospitality. There is not even the cleanliness that is essential for human dignity. Although most human beings experience disconcerting flashes of this domineering ego, very few persons remain focused on this level. Only war criminals and other enemies of humanity could be said to live primarily on the first level of consciousness. Nevertheless, there is nothing intrinsically evil about this first level. It provides a biological ground floor for human reality. Through this consciousness, the lungs breathe and the heart beats.

The second floor in the dream represents the critical or inquiring self. Most of humanity is focused on this level, where basic human refinements are beginning to appear. This dream imagery has nothing to do with social standing or affluence. There are persons living in presidential palaces who are occupying the dirt floor of the first level of consciousness, as well as persons who live in thatched huts who are enjoying the glorious palace of the fourth level of consciousness.

The evolutionary efforts carried on by this second level of the self constitute the critique of the domineering ego, the critique of selfish impulses. The search is carried on here for truly human and humane values, for disciplined and fruitful ways of life. There are many dimensions within this second level of consciousness. They are all essentially positive, honorable, and evolutionary, unless they remain dominated by the first level, obviously or subtly.

The third floor of this structure of consciousness is the fulfillment of our humanity. Human potential is here unfolded harmoniously. Perhaps the majority of human beings reach upper regions of the second level, but only excellent persons of good will become established on the third level. Here, ethical and religious ideals are in full flower. This level of development, or awakening to our true nature, is the real basis for civilization, religion, education, art, and science. Sincere seekers on the second level receive certain glimpses of the third level, but where one's awareness remains primarily focused is what counts for evolutionary development. In traditional Sufi parlance, the third level is the fulfilled or satisfied self.

One could reasonably inquire, how can there be levels higher than this fulfillment of human aspiration to an excellent, civilized existence? The four higher levels are the fruition of the mystic path of return. They are not, strictly speaking, part of human potential and human effort. They are the manifestation of Divine Reality through our human reality.

One usually must reach the third level of consciousness to receive authentic initiation into a mystical Order, or one may be

> "In the precious sacrament of dhikr, essential Divine Energies descend through the hearts and even through the physical bodies of the dervishes. Divine Reality becomes visible and experienceable as human reality."

lifted by Divine Grace, through this initiation, into the third level. When one reaches the fourth level, Divine Attributes begin to manifest directly and adorn the human being. This is symbolized in Rahima's dream as rare works of craftsmanship and art. These manifestations are not, however, works of human hands, nor are they brought about by human efforts. The transition to the fourth level usually occurs after physical death in the realm of Paradise consciousness. Only genuine mystics can generate enough spiritual intensity to enter this and higher levels during earthly experience. Once again, we recognize that gifted persons on the third level, or even on the second level, may receive glorious intimations of the fourth level of consciousness, but to be established there is an entirely different order of experience. Not even all the members of a mystical Order become established on the fourth level, which in traditional Sufi parlance is the tranquil self.

The fifth level is that of mystic union, where no finite modes of thought or perception operate, hence the symbol of total darkness. The thunderous music in the dream represents the Divine Resonance, from which universes are taking shape and into which finite existence disappears again. This was the only floor in the dream structure that caused Rahima nervousness and concern, since this radiant blackness is so far from our ordinary level of experience. In Sufi parlance, the fifth level is the peaceful self.

If we were to correlate the seven levels with the four steps, sharia would be the third level, tariqa the fourth, and haqiqa the fifth. The final two levels of consciousness are an expression of marifa, the astonishing dimension of spiritual manifestation that lies beyond mystic union. On the fifth level, there is only Truth and its Resonance. On the sixth level, creation appears once more, not through beautiful Divine Manifestations, as on the fourth level, but as the mystic crown, the sublime human form, symbolized by the circle of dervishes. One surprising piece of good news brought by Rahima's dream is the confirmation that the ancient ceremony of dhikr, traditionally conducted by candlelight, kneeling on sheepskins, actually affords the blessed dervishes in the circle a glimpse of the sixth level, although most of them may not even have become established on the fourth level. In the precious sacrament of *dhikr*, essential Divine Energies descend through the hearts and even through the physical bodies of the dervishes. Divine Reality becomes visible and experienceable as human reality. In Sufi terminology, the sixth level is the complete self.

The enigmatic seventh level of consciousness is a realm of brightness, clarity, subtle humor. The human form has been transcended, even as a mode of pure Divine Expression. Thus the seventh level resembles the fifth level in its absence of human reference. Yet here the imagery of light and luxurious growth replaces the imagery of mystic darkness. The human person of Rahima was not permitted to remain but was removed instantly in a playful and humorous manner. My Shaykh, Muzaffer Ashqi, used to comment simply, "On the seventh level of consciousness, if you imagine that you exist, it is idolatry." By the dynamic golden greenness of Supreme Reality, all possibility of the idolatrous perception of duality is tossed out the window. The colors on this seventh level indicate why Nureddin Jerrahi designated a golden cap wrapped in green cloth as the turban of his Order. Green is also the chosen color of the beloved Messenger of Allah. In Sufi parlance, the seventh level is the pure self.

Rahima was taken through this symbolic dream structure four times, indicating that she, although only twelve years old, was already in communion with the fourth level of consciousness. As she grows older, she will have to practice spiritual discipline and experience intense yearning to become fully established on this fourth level and to progress further. This dream is itself one of those rare works of Divine Art that manifested in the palatial fourth floor of her dream. Her unknown guide was probably Nureddin Jerrahi, may his spirit be sanctified, whose intercessory power, by the Permission and Foreknowledge of Allah, tenderly opened the way for this amazing dream, which has now become a channel of spiritual energy and illumination for us all, her grateful brothers and sisters.

Lex Hixon, Nur Al-Jerrahi, received his Ph.D. in World Religions from Columbia University in 1976. From about 1971 to the late 80's he conducted a weekly radio show in New York City called "In The Spirit," interviewing spiritual teachers from around the world. In the years that followed he entered into deep, serious study and practice of several of the world's religious traditions, eventually becoming a masterful teacher in some of them — including the western chapter of the Jerrahi Order of Istanbul with its several tekkas. Among his books are *Great Swan, Mother of the Universe, Heart of the Koran, Atom from the Sun of Knowledge, Mother of the Buddhas*, and *Living Buddha Zen*. For more information inquire at: **www.lexhixon.org** For ITS Series information inquire at: **www.srv.org**

Rabbi Eli Mallon ◆

PRAYER AND THE KNOWLEDGE OF G-D
Sacred Hymns of Enlightenment

The extraordinary dynamics of external and internal prayer are mapped out with clarity and sensitivity in the famous Jewish song, Adon Olam, whose devotional language and spiritual sentiments alone, when implemented with faith and understanding, are sufficient to usher one into the presence of the Divine.

Adon Olam is a popular synagogue song, typically sung at the conclusion of Shabbat and holiday morning services. It is traditionally ascribed to the great medieval poet Shlomo ibn Gabirol (Spain; 11th c.), although this has not been decisively determined.

Its metrical pattern allows for countless musical settings. Rarely, though, is close attention given to the words themselves. Over time, I came to realize that in its words, the poet — whoever he or she was — had perfectly outlined the process of contemplative prayer, as my experience of it has been.

The first verses declare abstract truths of G-d: Eternity; Unity; etc. This is how contemplative prayer begins — not with consideration of our own needs, or even with love for G-d. Rather, it begins with our profound acknowledgement of realities about G-d that are unchanging and utterly beyond ourselves. Immersing our attention in this brings us to profound quiet. This is our awe at the grandness of G-d.

When we give ourselves up to the contemplation of G-d, our soul takes us into a region beyond our present physical world. We transcend, we go beyond the limitation of finite thought, and we draw therefrom power, strength, and wisdom. If we have been nervous, tense, or worried, we can, in a few minutes, cause ourselves to become calm. It is a deliberate and conscious change from our daily thinking to a communication with the infinite, through our soul. It has been said that we can experience union with something larger than ourselves, a sense of oneness with the power beyond. In that union, we shall find our greatest contentment and peace. That union we make and can experience only through our soul.

We can "immerse our attention" in an idea when we stop "debating" it — arguing with ourselves whether we believe it or not — and begin to visualize the picture the idea paints. From that point, the key can be repetition.

Wave Hill is a beautiful, former mansion in Riverdale, NY, with grounds overlooking the Hudson River, that is now open to the public. Some years ago (having the time available during the summer, as a teacher), I would go there and sit in a chair, close my eyes, and for hours, simply repeat: "G-d is good, all is G-d, all is good." I made no effort to feel anything or to "concentrate." I made no effort to convince myself of the truth of this syllogism, either. I simply kept repeating the words. I would literally do this for hours. The longer I did it, the better I felt. Each day, if I started around 9:00 AM, by noon I was just overflowing with feeling blissful, secure; surrounded by, immersed in, and filled with G-d's Presence and Goodness. I thought I could not possibly feel any better. I could feel myself smiling. Seeing myself later in a mirror, I looked happier than I could remember appearing or feeling. Even so, after some days, something even greater happened: my heart began to burst with the same feeling. There was a real sense of getting to a new spiritual level. I thought my heart was already full (during meditation). What a surprise to find out that it was still "all in my head." What is more, it also began to permeate my feeling outside of these meditative times. This went on for a month. Of course, when school reopened, I hardly had the time to do this. Also, the daily pressures and frustrations increased, and I did not have as relatively peaceful a way of dealing with them as I do now (still need lots of progress in this area). I came to see the need for both the contemplative experience, and the learning of more peace-producing or maintaining responses. Although with enough contemplative experience, there would be a more or less natural transformation of responses, it is probably also true that along the way, we have to learn ways to not disturb the peace we receive in meditation.

When I returned to school, my principal remarked, "You look younger."

Jewish tradition offers other texts that can serve this purpose, too. But Adon Olam captures major themes in the tersest possible language.

The next verses affirm that our relation to this Infinite, almost unknowable, Presence is always a personal one. G-d is not simply a "Cosmic Being." G-d is "my G-d." G-d is not simply an abstract truth; G-d is a personal experience. The next stage in contemplation, then, after we have entered into G-d's Presence, is to affirm that G-d is not simply "there;" G-d is there for me. "My Rock." "My Redeemer in times of trouble." Our relation to G-d is the most intimate one imaginable. G-d is beyond the limits of anything finite, yet still nurtures even the smallest, least significant aspects of creation. This is the true nearness of G-d to us.

It is not for his or her own sake that the poet says 'my G-d...' Rather, it's the poet's way to tell us: this is your truth as well as mine. The poet is speaking our own words for us.

Having first affirmed that G-d's is the Presence in which we are and will always be; having then affirmed that our relation to this Presence is not a lifeless one, but one of deep intimacy and

> "G-d is not a thought or feeling; not matter or energy. G-d is beyond time and space. The entire Creation is less than a speck of dust compared to G-d. Thinking these, I begin to feel G-d's Silence. Now, I say: 'You are filling everything You are creating. Nothing is separate from You. There is only You.' I pause then from saying or thinking anything, my mind filled with Quiet. I cannot help telling G-d "I love You."

caring, the poet concludes with *"In G-d's Hands I put my soul…"* At this point, contemplation becomes "prayer;" especially "hitbodedut" (meditative prayer as practiced by Breslaver Hasidim). Whatever our need, whatever our concern, we give it to G-d. When we do, we are filled with a relief and a confidence that can not be described. If the first stage was primarily an intellectual one, and the second some combination of intellect and feeling, the third is utterly an act of the heart.

Praying, I first remind myself that G-d is creating everything right now. Everything is the effect; G-d is the cause. Then, I think: G-d is not a thought or feeling; not matter or energy. G-d is beyond time and space. The entire Creation is less than a speck of dust compared to G-d. Thinking these, I begin to feel G-d's Silence. Now, I say: 'You are filling everything You are creating. Nothing is separate from You. There is only You.' I pause then from saying or thinking anything, my mind filled with Quiet. I cannot help telling G-d "I love You." I feel You accepting my loving and Loving me in return. With Your help, I forgive anyone for whom I have an angry thought. They are your beloved children, too. Like an adult watching children be mean, thinking to Yourself, "Oy, how unnecessary," You love us no less. Now, I place my question or problem in my mind with You; "before You," some might say. I know you already know these, but by "saying" them, I can give them to You. If I keep them unspoken in my own mind and heart, I cannot let them go. It also helps me feel that I have shared them with You. I give them to You now. Maybe You give me an immediate answer; maybe the answer comes at some other time. Sometimes I have to pray about the same thing more than once until I can give it to You and let it go. I know that whatever You do is the best and rightest thing. Once I have given it to You, I feel much better. I have to say "I love You" again; I am so filled with the feeling. I finish my prayer, then.

But sometimes, even after I have opened my eyes, I still feel like I'm with You.

Adon Olam could be our main "script" for contemplation. In fact, it is a sequence that we go through almost spontaneously after a while.

If in our early attempts at personal prayer, we are naturally inclined to try the 3rd step first, we will probably find success at this to be intermittent, at best — a momentary, or temporary "letting go." It is the first two steps that allow us to move beyond haphazard spiritual experiences into something much more consistent and deep. They compel us to make permanent changes in our thinking.

Rabbi Joseph Gelberman was particularly inspired by the concluding line of the poem: *"G-d is for me; I will not fear."* His affinity for it grew out of formally and informally considering the earlier content of the poem for many years. It is not a fast process. It takes time and repetition. But we can truly progress in prayer and the direct, personal knowledge of G-d, by following the route mapped for us by *Adon Olam*. Even if we simply reflect on the steps, and naturally find ourselves developing our personal, private prayer, we will find them perfectly reflected in this poem's words.

G-d cannot be perceived through the mind alone. If you would know G-d, do not seek merely to prove His existence, but turn to Him with your heart; affirm your union with Him, affirm His responsiveness to prayer, pray to Him; if you actually turn to G-d, speak to Him in your heart, you will be astonished to find how close He is to you, you will feel His nearness, you will have found G-d.

Rabbi Eli Mallon, an educator and rabbi from the New York area, returned to Jewish learning after learning transcendental meditation in 1971. He has also practiced Yoga, Visualization (as taught at the Society of Jewish Science) and Johrei (a spiritual healing method from Japan, first taught by Mokichi Okada). His special area of interest is what Jewish tradition can teach us about personal and spiritual growth. www.rabbielimallon.wordpress.com

Stanzin Dawa ◆

POEM FOR HUMAN EXCELLENCE

I dedicate the following poem to the great master, Swami Vivekananda, who helps me and millions of others in understanding the essence and power of being human.

Today we have more universities but no higher Wisdom.
Today we have bigger temples but no human compassion.
Today we have bigger hospitals but no real health.
Today we have bigger factories but no secure employment.
Today we have bigger houses but no sense of family.
Today we have bigger bombs but no actual security.

Today we have more luxuries but no true comfort.
Today we have more money but no practical sense.
Today we have more religion but no abiding peace.
Today we have more civilization but no authentic culture.
Today we have more bridges but no clean water.

Today we have more leaders but no qualified followers.
Today we have more politics but no honest politicians.
Today we have more government but no wise governors.
Today we have more courts but no forthright justice.
Today we have more law but no underlying order.

Today we have more westernization but no modernization.
Today we have more cities but no surrounding forests.
Today we have more ships and armadas but no aquatic animals.
Today we have more aeroplanes but no birds of the air.
Today we have more speed but no clear direction.
Today we have more ignorance but no nullifying knowledge.

◆ David Escobar

INLAKECH

"You Are My Other Me."

The following article is Nectar's first offering from the Native American perspective. We have waited a long time to find a writer who has the permission of his people to write on spiritual values and practices. All world traditions have as their foundation indigenous perspectives and values with regard to our relationship with Nature and each other. In contemporary times these perspectives have been covered over in some cases, or the emphasis has shifted to transcendent perspectives. Yet, living in harmony and reverence with Nature, which includes gross and subtle levels or realms, is necessary for a balanced life and mind. This balance, in turn, is essential for the proper understanding of the spiritual wisdom in any tradition. For example, the ancient Vedic fire sacrifices, along with the five daily sacrifices to the gods, rishis, ancestors, humans, and other embodied beings, all purified and honed the heart and mind of the practitioner over time. Only when thus qualified would the guru or spiritual teacher bestow further teachings on the practitioner. As David Escobar writes below, the Lenca elders of Central America hold fast to this tradition and value as a means of preserving their spiritual culture. Thus, as Swami Vivekananda often prayed, may all beings become qualified in their respective traditions.

A few months ago, the Vedanta Society held its 2012 retreat in beautiful Olema, CA., and asked me to speak on Indigenous perspectives along with my own Lenca tribe's spirituality. Often, spirituality is a taboo subject among many Indigenous nations on the American continent, nevertheless I agreed. I was not sure what to expect, since it was my first time to speak before such a large crowd of people. As my gut suspected, all the congregants greeted me with love and kindness. Indeed, the greeting reminded me of my own community when I travel and visit Central America. Everyone gathers and celebrates the presence of a new visitor.

Where can I begin an article focused on indigenous spiritual perspectives, and not talk about the historical context? Somehow I must make an attempt to express the complex and diverse state of affairs for Indigenous peoples in the western hemisphere, as well as spiritual aspects without violating spiritual guidelines. What an order!

For starters, let us take a snapshot at the current issues within "Indian country." There are currently, over 560 nations that still exist in the Americas, along with thousands of languages still spoken today by peoples sometimes not seen or acknowledged and over 200 U.S/Indian treaties still not honored. Across the continents of the Americas, reservations, rancherias and villages suffer poverty, health issues, alcoholism, and high incidents of suicide. Children in South Dakota for example, still do their schoolwork under candlelight just like many of their counterparts in Mexico and South America. As I once mentioned to the prominent religious writer Houston Smith, "the thing that connects all Indigenous people together as I see it, is our mutual pain post first contact, and our interrelated connection to the Earth."

The other side of this legacy is the resiliency of Indigenous people and that of my own Lenca nation to resist and continue our way of life as best we can. Lately, there has been a resurgence of Indigeneity among youth and adults alike. However, we also have to understand that there has always been a maintenance and promotion of a living culture and spiritual beliefs. The question most people have is, how do "we" continue to do it?

Before I answer this question, it is important to put forth a disclaimer and mention that, I have received permission from the communities I come from to promote our Lenca culture here in the diaspora. Secondly, I do not, and will not speak, or represent the hundreds of Indigenous nations and their traditions that are present on this hemisphere. I am here simply to promote and educate regarding our Lenca way of being and the overall acknowledgement of Indigenous peoples. This notion of permission is a good segue into a basic instruction for Lenca peoples. As told long ago, anything I do in life must have permission, either from the Creator, Mother Earth, and/or from those elders who may have the wisdom for me to move forward with my endeavors.

This asking permission is one way that we as Lencas have been able to maintain our spiritual way and keep our culture alive. It is through our values that we see the outside world. "Permission giving" is a common value that is still practiced today among Lencas of Honduras and El Salvador and is called the "compostura" or the "fix."

For example, the action of asking permission before we plant or disturb the earth in any form is inextricably part of the Lenca value system. We believe that Creator spirit is contained in the entire natural world. As a traditional elder once said, we do not separate the Creator from the Creation. Our value lens, by which we see the world, contains not only the view but also the actions and conduct of ourselves in the natural world and with each other. Even maintaining and promoting our culture needs to have permission – yes, even our culture needs permission to exist. Another part of our values is the knowing that we are not in competition or are trying to subjugate our Mother.

One way to show how our way of life is still relevant today is by perhaps testing it. If we take one of the many energy-measuring tools that exist today on the commercial market, and place it near anything that comes from the natural world, we are able to see that the needle on that instrument moves and that ener-

> "In my opinion, the majority of industrial society has taken on a hamburger drive-thru approach to the sacred. The outer trappings of the teachings at times become more important than the teaching themselves. My Lenca elders have shown me that even as a grown Lenca man, I too must sit and wait for the understanding to come at its given time and place within my daily life. Ten years ago, I received a teaching, which only makes sense to me now in 2012."

gy is measurable. That object has energy or life; it is alive and holds power. Hence, that power stems from the Creator Him/Herself.

We, as Lenca peoples, believe that the Creator is not a fixed point and the energy He/She is, is not just above but everywhere from the smallest germ to the greatest mountain. From this perspective, we hold to be true a Meso-American pan-Indigenous concept of "Inlakech," which, translated means "you are my other me." This statement, I believe, holds a cosmological framework from which the majority of Indigenous peoples see the natural world. Our mental paradigm or cosmology is what makes us able to live and have a reciprocal relationship with our "Mother Earth"; it allows us to live a balanced life and have an understanding of how we are a part of the whole and no better or worse than everything else. Unfortunately, the West has not yet understood Inlakech. We as Lencas look at the evidence of history among the western world and can see that most of their prophets have been assassinated or jailed for teaching Inlakech. We as Lencas are perplexed by these actions.

Lenca and indigenous people still hold the ability to wait and have patience. It appears to me that many in the modern industrial mainstream society are in a rush to work, sleep, play, eat, and even pray. As some Indigenous youth and adults raised in urban areas begin to "re-indianize" themselves, I have learned, including for myself, that many of the spiritual concepts and principles must be spoon fed to us by those who have been born with "medicine" or have come into their "medicine," or spiritual wisdom.

These spiritual spoonfuls are not meant to be gulped down like a diet Pepsi. Spiritual teachings have to be swallowed gently just like a medicine. The medicine then integrates itself into our own spirit, personal cosmology, and daily life. This may take years or even an hour depending on each person's personal situation. However, this hurried way of life is where conflicts arise with the West's mainstream cosmology. In my opinion, the majority of industrial societies have taken on a hamburger drive-thru approach to the sacred. The outer trappings of the teachings at times become more important than the teachings themselves. My Lenca elders have shown me that even as a grown Lenca man, I too must sit and wait for the understanding to come at its given time and place within my daily life. Ten years ago, I received a teaching, which only makes sense to me now in 2012. Now, apparently was the right time and place to understand it.

Obviously, each teaching takes on a different meaning and result to the person receiving it, this may depend on the alignment both mentally, spiritually, and emotionally of that person. At least this has been the case with my own personal journey. In this same fashion, our oral tradition is something that Indigenous people hold dear to our hearts. It has been through our dedication in keeping our oral tradition alive that we Lencas and other Indigenous peoples have resisted colonialization and sustained our spiritual beliefs amidst the burning of our sacred texts or the killing of our spiritual leaders.

I will end here by sending a gentle voice out to all of the readers to continue to make connections daily, ask permission and see each other as "Inlakech," "you are truly my other me." We must lead by example and hold each other in both thought and prayer for the rough times that may lay ahead, for not only Indigenous people, but also all of humanity. Oheo!

David Escobar serves as a consultant specializing in cultural competency and sustainable indigenous wisdom and is the former Cultural Director of Three Nations Indian Circle and a member of the Bi-national Indigenous Council of El Salvador. He currently works for the Office of Fourth District Supervisor Steve Kinsey (Marin County, CA) where he is in the midst of facilitating farm worker housing in West Marin, a community garden in the Canal, and is the cofounder of Viviendo Verde Ya, an Indigenous Latino green campaign that is both local and Bay Area wide.

◆ *Dzogchen Ponlop Rinpoche*

Song from the Heart

Lineage Supplication to the Kagyu Gurus

Song from the Heart: The Lineage Supplication to the Kagyu Gurus, by Dzogchen Ponlop Rinpoche was presented as a public teaching at the Austin Shambhala Center in Austin, Texas, March 26, 2005.

Supplication to the Takpo Kagyu

Great Vajradhara, Tilo, Naro,
Marpa, Mila, Lord of Dharma Gampopa,
Knower of the Three Times, omniscient Karmapa,
Holders of the four great and eight lesser lineages—
Drikung, Tag-lung, Tsalpa, these three,
glorious Drukpa and so on—
Masters of the profound path of mahamudra,
Incomparable protectors of beings, the Takpo Kagyu,
I supplicate you, the Kagyu gurus.
I hold your lineage; grant your blessings
so that I will follow your example.

Revulsion is the foot of meditation, as is taught.
To this meditator who is not attached to food and wealth,
Who cuts the ties to this life,
Grant your blessings so that I have no desire
for honor and gain.

Devotion is the head of meditation, as is taught.
The guru opens the gate to the treasury of oral instructions.
To this meditator who continually supplicates him
Grant your blessings so that genuine devotion is born in me.

Awareness is the body of meditation, as is taught.
Whatever arises is fresh—the essence of realization.
To this meditator who rests simply without altering it
Grant your blessings so that my meditation
is free from conception.

The essence of thoughts is dharmakaya, as is taught.
Nothing whatever but everything arises from it.
To this meditator who arises in unceasing play
Grant your blessings so that I realize
the inseparability of samsara and nirvana.

Through all my births may I not be separated
from the perfect guru
And so enjoy the splendor of dharma.
Perfecting the virtues of the paths and bhumis,
May I speedily attain the state of Vajradhara.

The supplication to the Dakpo Kagyu lineage was written by a very diligent and great practitioner named Pengar Jampal Zangpo. He wrote it when he was practicing on a small island in a lake called Nam-tso, or "Sky Lake," in northern Tibet. That winter there was a very heavy snowfall and he got stuck on the island. During those days of intense practice and deep solitude, he sang this supplication that emerged from his heart.

What is the Lineage Principle?

The Lineage Supplication to the Dakpo Kagyu begins with a verse expressing the qualities of the lineage. The lineage principle is very important in Vajrayana. It has to do with keeping the instructions and the practice as authentic and genuine as possible. When such a lineage has been transmitted over many centuries, there is an element of preserving or passing down the enlightened wisdom itself. The lineage holders are the ones who hold the realization of the heart of enlightenment and transmit it to their disciples so that it continues throughout the centuries.

That is why the Kagyu lineage is especially known as "the lineage of true meaning." The "true" meaning referred to in that phrase is the ultimate or true nature of mind. When we realize the true nature of mind, we become capable of transferring that experience to the mindstreams of others. When that happens in an unbroken way, from one person to the next, it is what we call "lineage." It is just like lighting a candle flame — you have to hold some source of fire in your hand first before you can cause a candle to ignite and produce a flame. No matter how many beautiful mudras you perform in front of the candle, you will not be able to light it unless you first have some fire. Once one candle is lit, it can light many others.

That continuity is what we call "lineage." Therefore before the lineage can be passed down, the lineage holder must have this fire, this realization of the nature of mind, born in his or her own experience. After that the light of wisdom and enlightenment can be made available to other sentient beings so that they may illuminate their own hearts. We cannot supplicate properly unless we understand the lineage principle, the guru principle, and ourselves as students. This is very important.

The Guru Principle and Devotion

Those masters who have held such a lineage, then, become the object of our supplication. The guru, however, is not so easily defined. He or she is a big question mark, especially for our

Vajrayana path. There are a lot of complicated concepts going around about "guru." The best way to explain the guru principle, I think, is through an analogy: The guru is like a mirror, nothing more, nothing less. He or she is a mirror in which you see the reflection of your own face. A mirror has no fear of reflecting who you are. When you get up in the morning, the mirror shows you how you look at that moment. It doesn't shy away from reflecting you. It shows you what you need to fix. At the same time, the mirror does not stretch out a hand and offer to fix you. It does not tell you how to fix your hair or what clothes to wear. A mirror does not project anything. It simply reflects who you are. Ultimately what the guru is doing is reflecting your nature of mind. The enlightened mind that you see before you is a reflection of your own true nature of mind.

Furthermore, it is you who brings the mirror into your home; it does not walk into your house on its own. It is your choice what shape mirror you want — round, square, big enough to fill the whole wall, or something small — it is totally up to you. You can buy a mirror that is too big for your room, but you will not be able to use it. At the same time, you do not want something too small. You need something that fits your own situation. Where you hang the mirror is up to you as well.

Therefore, it is important to seek out a teacher who fits your own disposition, someone with whom you have a karmic connection. Making this connection is the same thing as bringing that mirror home. But then, even if you have the mirror, if there is no light, you can stand there in front of your mirror for ages and still not see anything. We cannot see without light. In the Vajrayana the light that helps us to see is the principle of devotion. If we turn on a light that is dim, we can only see some things dimly. So the brighter you shine your light, the clearer you can see the guru and the clearer you can see your nature of mind.

We must understand that the guru is not a savior. He or she is not someone you call to troubleshoot for you, someone who comes and fixes things and then goes away. It is not like that. The guru is simply like a mirror, and our devotion is like a light. With such a mirror and with such light we make this supplication that we may come to see the nature of our own mind.

The Three Kinds of Guru

Before we supplicate the guru, however, we should understand that there is more than one meaning of the term guru. There are three different kinds of guru that we can rely on — the outer, the inner and the ultimate.

The outer guru is an individual who holds an authentic lineage. This is the human master from whom we receive instructions and who guides us on our path of study, contemplation and meditation. He or she is the "mirror" with whom we are working.

The inner guru is the words of the Buddha, as recorded in the scriptures. While the outer guru is initially important, the inner guru eventually becomes very important as well. First, we meet the outer guru, who gives us the instructions that come from the lineage that arises from the wisdom of the Buddha. Next, however, we need to work with those instructions directly. It is this inner guru that leads us to an understanding of the outer guru's instructions and of how to work with them in our lives. If we did not pay attention to this inner guru, then our connection with our outer guru would just be like hanging out — like being a Dead-head who follows the Grateful Dead everywhere, partying and drinking and smoking. We cannot spend all our time at dharma parties, you know, following the guru everywhere as if we were fans. That is not the Buddhist way, the Vajrayana way. Of course it is important to have a personal connection with the guru, but once that is established, the most important thing is to put the instructions into practice. That is what we call "the inner guru."

Finally, the ultimate guru is related to the experience and realization of the true nature of mind. When you look at it, all the concepts we have of teacher, teachings and path, all the instructions, practices and ritual forms we learn, are still quite relative, still dualistic. Ultimately, what is most important is just to realize the truth, the true nature of mind, the dharmakaya mind. Therefore, the true guru, from the Vajrayana point of view, is your own nature of mind — and that is what we call "the ultimate guru." This is the guru we really rely on. Everything else is the relative guru. Therefore, ultimately speaking, this lineage supplication is invoking our own nature of mind.

The Kagyu Lineage

The Direct Lineage

The lineage supplication begins by invoking "*Great Vajradhara.*" Who or what is Vajradhara? Vajradhara is the primordial or Dharmakaya Buddha, the source of all manifestations of enlightenment, and the essence of the very nature of our mind.

Vajradhara is central to the Kagyu lineage. The great Indian mahasiddha, Tilopa, whom we supplicate next, demonstrated Vajradhara's unique significance to the lineage when he declared, "*I, Tilo, have no human guru — my guru is the Dharmakaya Vajradhara.*" Although Tilopa studied with many great masters, when he makes this statement, he is showing that, from an ultimate perspective, the real source of his transmission is the Dharmakaya Vajradhara, the absolute manifestation of Shakyamuni Buddha, and also the "ultimate guru." This transmission is what is called the "direct" lineage, or the "short" or "close" lineage.

The Indirect Lineage

There is an "indirect" or "long" lineage as well, which is traced back to Shakyamuni Buddha. It includes all of the students of the Buddha and all of their students, until you reach the time of Tilopa. It is composed of many individuals, among whom are the holders of the four special lineage transmissions.

Tilopa transmitted his lineage to the great Indian mahasiddha, Naropa. This begins the first great human transmission, from living master to student. Their relationship is quite famous and there are many stories about their years together. Naropa transmitted the lineage to his main student, who became known as Marpa, the Great Translator. Marpa, a Tibetan, crossed the

> "...grant your blessings so that I do not take honor and gain to be truly existent and therefore can let go of attachment to them. Grant your blessings so that I do not further my pride and mental afflictions by taking them to be real. Grant your blessings so that I may reverse my clinging in relation to them, so that I may feel revulsion toward them. This is a very profound supplication."

Himalayan Mountains three times on foot in order to study with his master, Naropa, in India. Traveling back and forth in this manner for over forty years, he finally brought the complete transmission of the lineage back with him to Tibet. Eventually he passed it to his student, Milarepa, the great tantric yogi of Tibet, who in turn passed it to his student, Gampopa.

Gampopa was the first Tibetan lineage holder who was a fully ordained monastic. He is called "the lord of dharma" because he unified the Mahamudra tradition of Milarepa's lineage with the stages-of-the-path tradition of the Kadampa lineage, thus establishing a unique stream of transmission known as the Dakpo Kagyu. When we say that we belong to the Dakpo Kagyu, that is a reference to the lineage of Gampopa, who is called "Dakpo Rinpoche" after his birthplace in the Dakpo region in southern Tibet.

From Gampopa the lineage was passed to the first Karmapa, Dusum Khyenpa, who is referred to in the supplication as the "knower of the Three Times, omniscient Karmapa." He became the founder of the Karma Kagyu lineage of Tibetan Buddhism, one of the main lineages in Tibet.

THE FOUR GREAT AND EIGHT LESSER LINEAGES
From Gampopa's Dakpo Kagyu, four main lineages developed:
  I. Barom Kagyu
  II. Tshalpa Kagyu
  III. Kamtsang or Karma Kagyu
  IV. Pakdru Kagyü

From the Pakdru Kagyu, developed eight additional Kagyu schools:
  1. Drikung Kagyu
  2. Taklung Kagyu
  3. Drukpa Kagyu
  4. Yasang Kagyu
  5. Trophu Kagyu
  6. Shuksep Kagyu
  7. Yelpa Kagyu
  8. Martsang Kagyu

Source: The Dzogchen Ponlop Rinpoche. "Introduction to Mahamudra" in The Ninth Gyalwang Karmapa, Wangchuk Dorje. Mahamudra: The Ocean of Definitive Meaning. Elizabeth Callahan, trans. Seattle: Nitartha international, 2001.

The Four Great and Eight Lesser Lineages

Within the Kagyu lineage there are four great lineages and eight branch lineages.

The four major Kagyu lineages are the Karma Kagyu, established by Dusum Khyenpa, the first Karmapa; the Tshalpa Kagyu; the Barom Kagyu; and the Pakdru Kagyu.

The additional eight "lesser" lineages (meaning subdivisions of its parent line) developed from one of the four major schools, the Pakdru Kagyu. This lineage was founded by the great master, Pakmo Drupa. Since he wrote many instructions and texts and taught extensively, he had more disciples than any of the other main lineage holders. Eventually other teachers developed within this main lineage, each with a different emphasis. Thus the Pakdru tradition branched off into eight subtraditions, or sublineages. Those eight became known as the eight lesser lineages: Drikung Kagyu; Taklung Kagyu; Drukpa Kagyu; Yasang Kagyu; Trophu Kagyu; Shuksep Kagyu; Yelpa Kagyu; and Martsang Kagyu

It may therefore be confusing that the text of the supplication says, "Holders of the four great and eight lesser lineages — Drikung, Tag-lung, Tsalpa, these three, glorious Drukpa and so on." Of these four, only one, the Tshalpa, is included in the four great lineages. The three others are included in the eight sublineages of the Pakdru. They are mentioned here because they were among the most famous of the lineages.

Among all these lineages, the most widely known is the Karma Kagyu lineage, which has been continued over the centuries through the impeccable activity of the Gyalwang Karmapas.

The Mahamudra Lineage

These lineages are the source of the "masters of the profound path of mahamudra" to whom we supplicate. They are what we call the lineage of Mahamudra. So, when we talk about the Mahamudra lineage, we are referring not just to one but to a great variety of Mahamudra teachings and lineages, all equally profound, all with great methods for realizing the nature of mind.

We supplicate to all these masters of the Mahamudra lineage because they are the "incomparable protectors" of all sentient beings. As practitioners of Mahayana Buddhism, we too aspire to help and protect sentient beings from suffering. How is such a thing accomplished? We can benefit sentient beings by creating an environment in which they can realize their nature of mind and develop compassion, loving-kindness and bodhichitta. What is so evident about these masters is that they have the profound skill of creating an environment in which disciples feel very easy, comfortable, and inspired to give rise to all this.

I supplicate you, the Kagyu gurus.
I hold your lineage; grant your blessings
so that I will follow your example.

As I have explained, when we supplicate, we must understand that we are not saying, "Please help me by taking me away from samsara, by taking away all my sorrows and causes of suffering." We are also not saying, "You are far above me, so you can save me. I am low and that is why I supplicate you to save me." That is not what we are doing here. What we are actually saying is, "I am supplicating you for inspiration. I aspire to hold your lineage and follow your example. I want to become like you — a realized, enlightened master — in order to realize the nature of mind and benefit sentient beings. Please grant your blessings by giving me the power and the positive environment in which to accomplish this."

The Practice of Mahamudra

The next few verses refer to the actual practice of meditation. First the common preliminaries are taught, then the uncommon preliminaries. The following two verses teach *Mahamudra shamatha* and *Mahamudra vipashyana*. The final verse comments on the topic of conduct, or discipline, and on the path to be traveled, which consists of the five paths and the ten bhumis.

Verse on the Common Preliminaries

If we want to cause Mahamudra meditation to arise in our mindstream, then we have to bring together the elements that will generate the most conducive and profound environment for it. If we want to grow something, we have to find fertile ground. The common preliminaries are the practice that plows that ground and prepares it for planting. Everybody likes to pick the fruit, but nobody wants to plow the field. The process of plowing the field is the toughest part of farming, and it is the toughest part of this journey as well. The common preliminary at the beginning of the Mahamudra path is renunciation, which is spoken of here as revulsion.

Revulsion is the foot of meditation, as is taught.

Revulsion is like the foot of meditation because without feet we cannot go anywhere. Similarly, if we do not have revulsion for samsara, then we are lacking the means of support that will carry us forward and lead us to meditation and to any possible progress on the path. Therefore this master, Pengar Jampal Zangpo, is teaching us that the first preliminary practice on the path to Mahamudra is to generate the heart of renunciation. This is very important. Once we generate that heart of renunciation, we will naturally be freed from our attachment to this life's enjoyments. This is what we need to relinquish — our attachments to this life.

To this meditator who is not attached to food and wealth,
Who cuts the ties to this life,

This line could equally be translated, "*who cuts the rope of attachment to this life.*" It is not saying that we need to throw everything related to this life away. Rather, it is saying that we need to relinquish our attachment to the appearances of this life. It is important to make this distinction. It does not mean that we have to renounce the world and everything in it and go somewhere else. Where would we go? Instead it is referring to cutting our fixation, attachment, and clinging to the enjoyments of this worldly life. It is our neurotic clinging that is actually causing our suffering and confusion.

As Tilopa said to Naropa, "*Son, you are not bound by appearances, you are bound by clinging. Cut through clinging, Naropa.*" This is a very pithy and powerful statement. In a similar vein, Shantideva, in the chapter on wisdom in the *Bodhicharyavatara*, or The Way of the Bodhisattva, said, "*We do not wish to refute appearances; what is to be reversed is thinking of them as being real.*" He also said, "*Nor do we wish to block off what we see and hear. What we wish to stop is the cause of suffering: thinking of these as being real.*"

You can understand this quite well from the example of a dream. When you are dreaming and do not recognize that you are dreaming, that dream can produce a lot of suffering. Why? If in your dream you see tigers, rattlesnakes, or even more ferocious beings, such as humans, and you take them to be real creatures that truly exist outside of you, then you will experience great fear. When you run from them, they will chase you. If you think that they truly exist "out there" and you truly exist "here," then the very strength of your dualistic fixation and clinging will cause your suffering to increase.

But in the very moment that you recognize you are dreaming, your dream becomes a lucid dream. You realize, "Oh, I am actually just dreaming," and you see that there is no real tiger out there and no real "me" here, and therefore all your fear and sufferings dissolve. There is no more samsaric pain and no chasing game. If, at that moment, you do not wake up but continue to have a lucid dream, then you can continue to engage with those dream appearances, which are simply appearance-emptiness. In that way you can accomplish whatever you wish, without any fear, pain, or suffering.

Therefore, when we generate revulsion and cut through the ties of desire to this life, what we are actually doing is cutting through our clinging to the appearances of this life as being real. We are not trying to forsake the appearances but to recognize that that is really all they are — mere appearances. So we make the following supplication:

Grant your blessings so that I have no desire
for honor and gain.

In other words, grant your blessings so that I do not take honor and gain to be truly existent and therefore can let go of attachment to them. Grant your blessings so that I do not further my pride and mental afflictions by taking them to be real. Grant your blessings so that I may reverse my clinging in relation to them, so that I may feel revulsion toward them. This is a very profound supplication.

This verse is a reference to one of the common preliminaries, which also includes the Four Reminders, the reflections on precious human birth; on impermanence and death; on karma, cause and effect; and on the shortcomings of samsara. All of these help us to develop renunciation, or revulsion.

Verse on the Uncommon Preliminaries

The third verse is a bold reference to the uncommon preliminaries.

Devotion is the head of meditation, as is taught.

Devotion — to the guru, the lineage and the teachings — is like the head of meditation in Mahamudra. In fact it is said that Mahamudra is actually the path of devotion. This devotion is based on confidence. It is the confidence that comes from understanding the lineage, understanding the teachers and the lineage gurus, and understanding the importance of realizing these teachings. From this we develop faith and devotion.

When we work with devotion, we are really working with our emotions. On the basis of this heart of devotion, many difficult emotions arise — passion, jealousy, aggression, and so on. These emotions may arise quite vividly due to our hope and fear in relation to our teacher, or because we are comparing our own style of devotion or accomplishments in practice to the styles and accomplishments of our fellow dharma practitioners. When we work with these mental afflictions in relation to devotion, it becomes a very powerful way of transcending them.

The guru opens the gate to the treasury of oral instructions.

There are many profound Vajrayana, Mahamudra, and Dzogchen teachings, and when you read them or even practice them, it is possible to understand many of them to a certain degree. However, without a guru's oral instructions, true understanding and practice become very difficult. The guru's instructions are like the key or the password that opens the gate to this vast body of infinitely profound teachings, instructions and experiences. Therefore without the guru and his or her oral instructions, the scriptures of Vajrayana, Mahamudra, and Dzogchen are not very effective.

Furthermore, many of these key instructions on the essential points of practice of Mahamudra, Dzogchen, and Vajrayana have never been written down. Some masters with whom I have studied will not allow you to write them down. You are expected to just listen directly to their instructions and then practice them. After that you go back and engage in many question-and-answer sessions — only you don't get to ask the questions. They ask you the questions!

With this understanding and sense of appreciation, we continually supplicate the guru that genuine, uncontrived devotion may be born in our minds. Devotion is a very powerful element of our path. I have experienced its power myself in relation to working with my own devotion toward my gurus, His Holiness the Sixteenth Karmapa, His Holiness Dilgo Khyentse Rinpoche, and Khenpo Tsultrim Gyamtso Rinpoche. It is a very powerful experience — very colorful and painful. Yet, at the same time, it is full of joy.

Verse on Mahamudra Shamatha

In the next verse, we look at the actual practice of Mahamudra.

Awareness is the body of meditation, as is taught.
Whatever arises is fresh—the essence of realization.
To this meditator who rests simply without altering it

The key point in Mahamudra shamatha meditation is simply not to be distracted. If we were to translate the Tibetan literally, we would say, "Nondistraction is the body of meditation, as is taught." Therefore, nondistraction — simply not being distracted by any outer or inner conditions — is what shamatha meditation is all about. Thus, if you are not distracted in the moment-to-moment experience of your daily life, then Mahamudra shamatha is there. If you are on the cushion in the shrine room and are not distracted, then Mahamudra shamatha is there as well. This mere nondistraction is what is being put forth as meditation.

If you would like to take up the practice of meditation, then it is not all that important to exert yourself in anything else. In that case, the most important thing is simply not to be distracted. Whatever thoughts arise, whatever emotions or mental afflictions arise, their fresh essence, their fresh nature, is what we rest upon here. We are not looking for another place to rest. Where we are trying to rest our mind is in the nature of this fresh, presently arising moment of mind, whatever it is. If our present mind is a thought, then we rest in the fresh essence of that thought. If our present mind is an emotion, such as anger, then we rest our mind in the fresh essence of that anger.

From the Mahamudra point of view, one of our greatest obstacles is doubt. Sometimes we think, "Mahamudra is not really working for me. I will look for something else. Maybe Dzogchen." But after we have practiced Dzogchen for a while, we encounter the same thing: "Oh, Dzogchen is not really working. I will look for something else. Oh, yes! Mahamudra." We go around and around, and this is what we call samsara — constantly cycling around and around.

Therefore, not looking anywhere else, or for something else, outside of our present mind, we just rest in this present nature of mind. This is Mahamudra shamatha. Without changing this present experience, we just rest in its essence, its nature. We do not have to make this thought better; we do not have to make it worse. We do not have to invite more thoughts; we do not have to reject the thought we have now. We simply rest in its freshness.

We can understand this a little better if we look at the line *"Whatever arises is fresh — the essence of realization."* Here the word realization is tok-pa (*rtogs pa*) in Tibetan. Now, depending on how you spell it, it can mean two different things, yet both words sound exactly the same. One of them means "thought" (*rtog pa*), while the other means "realization" (*rtogs pa*). The translation of tok-pa here refers to realization, but in most cases, the word is understood to mean thought. If it were the latter, the line would mean, "In the fresh essence of whatever thoughts arise . . . ." That, then, is what we would rest in. So we could say, "To this meditator who rests simply in the fresh essence of whatever thoughts arise." In the end, however, the meanings are actually the same. Whatever thoughts arise, their freshness is the essence of realization. When you look at that essence, it is realization. There is no realization outside that thought.

The Mahamudra teachings say that what obstructs us most

from seeing the nature of our mind is simply that we keep looking for it outside our mind, outside our experiences. For that, Mahamudra uses the following example: It is like searching for one's buffalo. Let us say you are a farmer who owns a buffalo. Not knowing that your buffalo is in its stable — having missed that fact — you suddenly freak out, thinking, "I've lost my buffalo. It's not in my stable. Where is it?" So you start frantically looking for your buffalo. Of course, when you first start looking, you see buffalo tracks everywhere. When you go beyond your own property, you might see some tracks that lead you to a nice cave in the Himalayan Mountains. You are certain to find a nice buffalo up there! The problem is, however, that when you do find that buffalo, you realize it is not your buffalo. It does not recognize you and you do not recognize it. It is Milarepa's buffalo that you find in the Himalayas. Likewise, you can follow another set of tracks to the riverbanks of the Ganges, and you will surely find a buffalo there — a nice, relaxed buffalo resting on the banks of the Ganges River — but again, the problem is that it is not your buffalo. That buffalo belongs to Tilopa. And since it belongs to Tilopa, it may kick you quite hard!

So you keep searching and searching, and eventually you give up your hope of finding your buffalo, and you give up your fear of losing your buffalo. Then you say to yourself, "What the heck, I'm going home." And once you come home, you find your buffalo. It had never wandered off. It was there all along, sitting relaxed and happy inside your stable. When you first find your buffalo, when you first see it again, that meeting is so powerful, so romantic. You look at your buffalo, and your buffalo looks at you, and you recognize each other. You both feel the bond. Finding your own buffalo is different from finding someone else's buffalo. Finding your own enlightenment is different from finding someone else's enlightenment.

Therefore, the Mahamudra teachings are telling us not to look outside, because the buffalo is always at home. The nature of mind is always at home, in this present mind. What is this present mind? Present mind is all of our thoughts, all of our emotions, all of our feelings that we are experiencing right now. If you keep looking outside this present mind, you will never find the nature of mind.

When we say, "Do not look outside," this does not mean, "Do not look outside your body." Rather, it means, "Do not look outside the experience of this present mind." So this verse on Mahamudra shamatha is saying, "Rest in this present mind as freshly as possible, as directly and nakedly as possible, and as free of contrivance as possible."

*Grant your blessings so that my meditation is free
from conception.*

Here we are supplicating that our meditation will not be altered or obscured by our thoughts or conceptions and that, as a result, we will be able to directly realize the true nature of mind. The word conception here means the dualistic conception of believing there is a meditator, on the one hand, and something to meditate on, on the other. It also refers to the mind of dullness and torpor. So here we are aspiring to be free from all such forms of dualistic fixation and dullness. If we are free from these two, then we will experience genuine Mahamudra shamatha.

Verse on Mahamudra Vipashyana

Next is the verse that explains Mahamudra vipashyana:

*The essence of thoughts is dharmakaya, as is taught.
Nothing whatever but everything arises from it.
To this meditator who arises in unceasing play*

All our thoughts and emotions are like the waves on the ocean. The ocean itself is dharmakaya mind, the wisdom of buddha. Just as waves arise from the ocean and dissolve back into the ocean, all of our thoughts and emotions arise from the expanse of wisdom and dissolve back into it.

As it says here, the essence or true nature of thoughts is dharmakaya mind. There is no wisdom outside the true nature of our thoughts, the true nature of our emotions. Where it says, "Nothing whatever . . ." we could instead say, "it is nothing whatsoever . . ." because, when we look at the essence of our thoughts, we cannot identify what we are seeing as being one thing or another since it does not truly exist. When you penetrate the essence of thought, when you look nakedly at its essence, then it is spacious and expansive. It has no solid or truly existing characteristics. It is free from all our concepts of what thought is.

And yet, thoughts appear in a variety of forms. They can appear as anything. Even though their essence, when examined, is found to be empty, it arises with great luminosity, great clarity, in every possible form. That it arises "as anything" shows us the very strong clarity or luminous aspect of the essence of thought. That is why it says here, *"everything arises from it."*

This stream of luminosity that is the essence of thoughts is unceasing. It is the unceasing play of the luminous nature of mind. Therefore the more strongly we experience a thought, the more vividly we are experiencing this luminous nature of mind. It is the same with the emotions. When you feel an emotion such as intense anger, if you can really look at its essence, it is beautiful. It gives you great strength, great power to realize this luminous nature of mind.

This verse teaches that when we look at the essence of thought, the fact that it does not exist in any form shows its dharmakaya, or emptiness, nature. Nonetheless it arises and manifests as luminous forms with tremendous energy, and this reveals its sambhogakaya nature. Furthermore, this luminous manifestation is unceasing. Whether we are walking or resting, whether we are attending to or oblivious of our thoughts, they continue in an unceasing play. That is their nirmanakaya nature. Therefore thoughts are taught to be in the nature of the three kayas, which are the three inseparable aspects of the enlightened nature of mind.

*Grant your blessings so that I realize the inseparability
of samsara and nirvana*

As the text says, if we realize the essence of thoughts, we will have realized the inseparability of samsara and nirvana. That is so because samsara and nirvana are only thoughts. The distinction between samsara and nirvana is created by thoughts and nothing else. Confused thoughts are what are called "samsara," and the mere end of that confusion is what is called "nirvana."

Therefore, samsara and nirvana are only established on the basis of thoughts. If we realize the dharmakaya that is the essence of thoughts, we will realize that neither samsara nor nirvana truly exists. And that is what we call "the inseparability of samsara and nirvana."

This verse echoes what Milarepa constantly taught. He said that the three essential points, or three stages, of practicing Mahamudra vipashyana are to *"look nakedly, rest directly, and relax at ease."* This means that whatever thoughts or mental afflictions we might be experiencing, we should look at their essence nakedly, directly, without trying to change them or fix them in any way. And right within that looking, we should rest. When we are resting, we must not fixate on that resting but rather relax at ease.

In fact, relaxation is taught to be an extremely important element of practice. It is said in the Kagyu lineage that from excellent relaxation comes excellent meditation, from middling relaxation comes middling meditation, and from lesser relaxation comes lesser meditation. Thus relaxation is the key to Mahamudra, as well as Dzogchen, meditation.

Through all my births may I not be separated
from the perfect guru
And so enjoy the splendor of dharma.
Perfecting the virtues of the paths and bhumis,
May I speedily attain the state of Vajradhara.

It would be great if we could attain buddhahood in this lifetime, but just in case we do not, the verse begins with the phrase *"Through all my births."* We might say that this is our plan B. As Vajrayanists, our plan A is *"in this lifetime."*

In the line *"May I not be separated from the perfect guru,"* the term "perfect guru" refers to a "fully qualified guru." What makes a fully qualified guru? Milarepa taught this in brief when he said, *"What defines a lama is that he or she holds a lineage."* Therefore, a fully qualified lama or guru is one who holds the lineage.

The next line says, *"And so enjoy the splendor of Dharma."* This lets us know that it would not be sufficient for us just to be connected to the guru. We also need to receive dharma teachings from him or her. This is a very good line because it shows very clearly what the path is. It is not enough just to become a good fan of a good guru. We must study and practice too. *"Perfecting the virtues of the paths and bhumis"* refers to the five paths and the ten bhumis, or bodhisattva grounds. Finally, the line, *"May I speedily attain the state of Vajradhara"* refers to the state of buddhahood, or complete awakening, and to the swift accomplishment of that goal.

When we connect with our heart of devotion in this way, then, in that moment, we are connecting very powerfully, immediately and directly with the awakened heart of the guru and the lineage, as well as our own inherently awakened state. We are not just relying on our own efforts. We are opening ourselves to a source of blessings that is an embodiment and a reflection of our own fundamental nature. When we genuinely supplicate the guru and the lineage, we feel the presence of the sacred world; the qualities of clarity, gentleness, peace, joy, and equanimity are naturally with us.

Dzogchen Ponlop Rinpoche is a widely respected teacher known for his skill in making the full richness of Buddhist wisdom accessible to modern minds. He is also a poet, visual artist and city-dweller, based in the United States for two decades. He devotes much of his energy to developing a vision of a genuine Western Buddhism that is free from the cultural hang-ups that distract us from the Buddha's essential message of wakefulness. He is the founder and principal teacher of Nalandabodhi, an international network of Buddhist practice centers, and Nitartha International, an educational non-profit devoted to the preservation of Buddhist literature and art. Nalanda West, Center for American Buddhism, in Seattle. His latest book is Rebel Buddha (Shambhala Publications).
twitter.com/ponlop
www.facebook.com/DzogchenPonlop
www.dpr.info.

Paravasta Sam Bailey

SPIRITUAL DISCERNMENT
Across the Spectrum of World Religious Traditions

Spiritual Discrimination, *viveka,* is the proper and necessary beginning to authentic spiritual life. Without it the practitioner is very probably not one at all. We have heard that, before coming to America, and while wandering the Indian subcontinent, Swami Vivekananda was calling himself Swami Satchitananda. It is very possible that, coming to know of the crying need for clear discernment in the world — at religious, philosophical, and spiritual levels — he donned the name of Vivekananda in order to demonstrate its inestimable value and efficacy. May the difference between the Real and the unreal dawn on all minds.

The subject of this article is the universal nature of spiritual discrimination, in both its affirmative and negative phases, across the spectrum of world religious traditions. Vedantists will be familiar with the idea of discrimination between the Real (God) and the unreal (projected world of sense experience). The essence of this idea is perfectly encapsulated in the sacred phrase *"Brahman Satya Jagat Mithya"* or *"The world is unreal, God alone is Reality."* As already mentioned, its practice has two phases.

The World is Unreal

The first, or negative phase, is that of negating the unreal world that we falsely superimpose by our ignorance as a veil that obscures the pure, Divine Essence, which alone is. This is called *"neti neti"* or *"not this, not this."* It can be applied to any substance or object, movement or vibration, thought, image, impression, or feeling; in short, anything that undergoes change and is impermanent, and therefore cannot be the Self, or God.

The idea here is that as we examine each and every thing that falls within the domain of sense experience, asking ourselves "Is this the Self?" for each sense object we encounter, we will discover that the answer is: "not this; this is not the Self." We follow this process until every obscuring veil has been negated, revealing that unique, partless, and indivisible Reality that depends upon nothing for Its own existence.

The result of taking such an enquiry into Existence itself to its ultimate conclusion will be that every direction we might turn, we will see the face of God. We have given a sense of reality to all these mundane things within the fleeting realm of sense experience for far too long. Therefore, we begin the process of Yoga by negating the idea of permanency and true reality in them. The reason we do this is to know the Lord, the true Reality, Who is the Substratum behind them all. It is to *"Strip the wrappings off the Gift"* as Babaji Bob Kindler has said in his poem, *We are Atman All-Abiding.* We are to come to know that all along it was God who was in all these things.

The changing outward forms, or *Vikriti,* we accepted as real; but where is true Reality for unstable forms that are manifest today and then gone tomorrow, vanished like a wisp of smoke? Because of their impermanence, trying to find happiness in material objects is like trying to walk across quicksand, hoping it will be stable enough to support our weight until we reach the other side, what to speak of our journey across the great, Mayic ocean of worldly existence. Therefore, we see that it is wiser to seek for That which is Changeless, and cleave to That instead.

Material form, of itself, is insubstantial. Even in the world of science, quantum mechanics has "firmly" established this. Rather, Existence itself is the true Substance behind all form. Enquiry into this basic truth is what is called Viveka, or Discrimination, and it is inseparable from *Tyaga,* Renunciation. In the deeper, existential sense, this is Divine Scientific Enquiry.

Renunciation as Discrimination

Concerning renunciation, Bhartrihari has said *"Enjoyments of embodied beings are fleeting, like the quick play of lightning within a mass of clouds; life is as insecure as a drop of water attached to the edge of a lotus leaf and dispersed by the wind; the desires of youth are unsteady; realizing these quickly, let the wise firmly fix their minds in Yoga, easily attainable by patience and equanimity."* (Vairagya Satakam, v. 35)

In his Gospel, Sri Ramakrishna has shown that this teaching is also at the heart of the Gita revelation: *"The Divine Mother has revealed to me the essence of the Vedanta. It is that Brahman alone is real and the world is illusory. The essence of the Gita is what you get by repeating the word ten times. The word becomes reversed. It is then 'tagi,' which refers to renunciation. The essence of the Gita is: 'O man, renounce everything and practice spiritual discipline for the realization of God.'"* (Gospel of Sri Ramakrishna, p. 255)

And what is the reward of renunciation? Lord Jesus explained it most beautifully: *"Assuredly, I say to you, there is no one who has left house or parents or brothers or wife or children, for the sake of the Kingdom of God, who shall not receive many times more in this present time, and in the age to come, eternal life."* (Luke 18:29-30; Orthodox Study Bible)

God Alone is Real

This brings us to the second or affirmative phase of discrimination, which is called *"iti iti"* or *"all this, all this."* The idea is that once we have clearly seen the insubstantiality of outward forms, we may finally see that *"what existed was the Lord Himself,"* to quote Swami Vivekananda. We realize that in their essence, all these things are but God's appearance through the veils of time, space, and causation. We see them in their true nature. This relative world we call nature is like a mirror which but reflects God's glory, expressing the overflow of *Ananda*, or the bliss of Brahman, absorbed in His own perfect Self-Aware nature.

I have heard it said that this affirmative phase of discrimination is not necessarily an active effort on our part, but more the vision of Unity that naturally shines forth without effort once we have removed the obstructing clouds of ignorance from our minds by the practice of discrimination. From the Sufi point of view, the first or negative phase of discrimination is that in which, turning away from the world, we take one faltering but committed step toward God, with faith. Now, this second or affirmative phase would be when, after our initial and limited step, we realize that God is rushing with one hundred steps to embrace us.

"Iti iti" is not a spiritual practice per se, but rather, the actual state of Realization. That it is not an effect based on spiritual striving as a cause fits perfectly with the experience of realized souls who can state, based on their realization, that personal agency is an illusion. One does not effect one's own realization by personal actions. One cannot cause what already is. Jivatman is already Paramatman. Jiva is already Siva. And how can the particular be said to be a cause for the general, which is its own substratum, and from which it arises and within which its own existence participates in Being?

From this point of view, even the initial phase of negating the unreal cannot truly be said to be caused by the Jiva or the individual soul. It is Brahman alone who is the actor upon this universal stage. From the standpoint of the Infinite, the jiva does nothing; the sole Agent in back of universal activity is Brahman (or universal subjectivity).

This is the true meaning behind the modern Christian idea that Divine Grace and spiritual self-effort are mutually exclusive principles. Taken within the non-dual context, this Christian idea is perfectly true. But when it is not correctly understood, it does not take into account the larger picture, and therefore in taking a one-sided approach to the problem, the fact of suffering is not effectively dealt with.

For as long as one remains within the dream, or Maya, one cannot truly claim the knowledge of either the waking state or Reality. One must start from where one is, and this is only made possible by moving in stages of ascending awareness from the gross material world to the subtlety of the spiritual Reality which is its foundation. And this does not happen without spiritual striving. Therefore, Sri Ramakrishna has said, *"The wind of God's Grace is always blowing, but one must raise one's sail to catch it."*

There are many clear signs that this practice of discrimination is not only crucial to true religion, but is a universal phenomenon that manifests in various ways among the world's religious traditions. More recently, this idea began to take deeper root in my consciousness while I was reading from a holy scripture of the Divine Mother called the *Srimad Devi Bhagavatam*. Below is the passage that sparked my imagination, giving rise to this fruitful inquiry. It relates an amazing story, upon reading which, I was struck, not only with its profound meaning, but also that its teaching relates the same essential meaning as the Islamic *zikr* phrase *"La ilaha il' Allah,"* *"There is nothing other than God!"*

The Divine Mother Teaches Discrimination

Here is the story: "O Child! In days of yore, at the end of an age, Bhagavan Hari (Sri Krishna) was lying as a small child on a floating leaf of a Banyan tree, and was thinking thus: 'Who is the Intelligent One that has created me a small child? What is his purpose? Of what stuff am I made? And how am I created? Whence can I know all this?' At this moment, the Devi Bhagavati, who is Consciousness Itself, seeing the high-souled Bhagavan Hari musing thus, spoke out in the form of a celestial voice in the following half-stanza: 'All this that is seen is I Myself; there is existent nothing other that is eternal.'" (tr. Swami Vijnanananda)

There is certainly more to this Bhagavata story, but it will suffice to say that by the time I reached the statement *"All this that is seen is I Myself; there is existent nothing other that is eternal,"* I had chills running up and down my spine. I had learned long ago that if this happens, especially when I am reading some passage of sacred scripture, it is often a good idea to pay close attention! In this particular instance, I was immediately cognizant that this half-stanza has the same meaning as the Islamic zikr phrase, *La ilaha il' Allah*, which is often translated as *"There is no God but God,"* but which the Sufis more appropriately take to mean, *"There is nothing save God."* The word *"zikr"* (sometimes spelled *dhikr*) which designates this sacred Islamic phrase, means Remembrance; in particular, remembrance of our identity with God, alone in which our true identity may be found, or rediscovered from beneath the veils which the ego (the Sufis call this *Nafs*) projects to conceal the Divine Reality within.

Jesus Christ, revered by the Sufis as *"Issa Ruh' Allah"* or "the very Breath of God" has expressed it in this way: *"The Kingdom of Heaven cometh not with sense perception, for lo, the Kingdom of Heaven is within you."* Therefore, if as Jesus has said, the Kingdom of Heaven is the Divine Reality within us, then dualistic sense perception, allegorically referred to in the book of Genesis as the tree of the knowledge of good and evil, is the veil that conceals it.

Turning again to the Srimad Devi Bhagavatam story, one can see in the divine utterance of the Mother of the Universe, the same negative and affirmative phases which we see in the practice of neti neti and its nondual result, or iti iti. One can take contemplation of this passage and its meaning as a clear and concentrated form of that same kind of discrimination. But it is also to be seen that not only does this teaching of the Mother share an inner meaning with the Islamic *zikr* phrase, but that the *zikr* also contains the same negative and affirmative phases of discrimination. Thus, the Devi says, *"all this that is seen,"* meaning anything phenomenal, or that can be part of our sense experience, whether internal or external, subtle or gross. To complete this idea, *"all this that is seen is I Myself"* is affirmation of Reality, of true Existence. She also says *"there is existent nothing other,"* which tells us that She is the Divine Substratum in which all objects and beings subsist, or as St. Paul says, *"In Him we live and move and have our being."* The Mother is Infinite, Absolute Existence; therefore, what else can exist but Her? As the Sufis say, there is nothing save God. All things relative exist only as God's expression. Nothing can exist outside the Mother, She being Existence itself. So She says, *"nothing other...."*

That Divine Being, conceived as the Heavenly Father in the Old Testament, restates the very same age-old truth within a Semitic context when He says, *"Thou shalt have no other gods before Me."* Of course, the inner meaning of this verse is what needs understanding, not the literalist interpretation which gets mired in trying to express the Eternal and Undivided Being through inherently dualistic reasoning and language. The *"other gods"* spoken of here mean the idols of false conception, appearance, and identity.

In Sufic terminology, it is the universal attributes or *"Sifat Allah,"* which have no inherent self-existence, but rather depend upon Allah for their expression, and belong to Him alone. To come full circle, this divine statement of Truth, expressed in various ways, is also mentioned in another form at the beginning this article, as *"The world is unreal, God alone is real."* As the *Sifat* or Divine Attributes depend upon *Allah* for their expression, so is this world appearance real only in that God is its foundation.

Furthermore, from the standpoint of Yoga, when the yogini meditates upon the alambanas, or perceptual constituents of the universe such as earth, water, fire, etc., as insubstantial, instead taking God to be their true basis, she is negating these *"other gods"* to know that *"The Kingdom of Heaven lies within."* In other words, to use Christian terminology, she has put aside her idols.

Now for the last part of the Divine Mother's statement in the Devi Bhagavatam. *"There is existent nothing other that is eternal"* means that what is relative, which is to say any thing or any being that is part of phenomenal, conditioned existence, is but a passing display, an impermanent appearance that both expresses and at the same time veils that divine Substratum which is the basis for its manifestation. What is Real is not the passing appearances, but the Divine Essence which allows them their day in the sun, so to speak.

Islam Teaches Discrimination

The following is how the two parts of the Mother's statement correlate to the two parts of the Islamic affirmation of the Divine Unity:

(1) The first part of the zikr is *"La ilaha,"* which in essence means: *"There is nothing that is not Allah."* The Sufis call the state of total immersion in the ocean of God's existence *"Fana,"* or Annihilation in God. I remember one Sufi teacher saying that this phase is like sweeping away the dead, dried up leaves of false identity. On reflection, one can see a clear correspondence with the second part of the Mother's statement, that *"There is existent nothing other that is eternal."* M. P. Pandit expressed it thusly: *"All that exists is That, for there can be nothing besides it."* (Gems from the Tantras). Each of these statements in their respective contexts negates all that is unreal. But then, what is left? God alone, or as Sufi Hazrat Inayat Khan has said, *"The Only Being."*

(2) The second part of the *zikr* is *"il' Allah,"* which in essence means: *"Everything is Allah."* This is hardly different from the first part of the Mother's statement, that *"All this that is seen is I Myself."* It is an unqualified statement of the truth of Absolute Bliss. The Sufis would say that back of *Sifat Allah* or the Divine Attributes, which can be seen in expression throughout the creation, is *Zat (Dhat)*, or God's Divine Essence. When, by God's Grace, this is realized, *Baqa* is the state of subsistence or life in God.

It is telling that often during this phase of the *zikr* chant, the head traces a straight line downward, to the center of the heart. What is implied, of course, is that inward Reality which lies within, at the center of all things, as their true being. Again, M.P. Pandit offers further clarification: *"This universe too is the Divine, a form of the Divine Puissance that has brought it into being from out of the Infinite. It is not so much a creation as an emanation from the Divine Being. It has the same substance intrinsically as the Divine.... Basically all is divine in character...."* (Gems from the Tantras)

Shaykh Ibrahim Gasur-i-ilahi, in his book on the teachings of the Sufi saint, Mansur al-Hallaj, says: *"Here you should lose your 'self' and search for your lost 'self' in Existence."* (The Secret of Ana'l Haqq: Muhammad Ashraf Publishers) *"Here you should lose your 'self,'"* corresponds to the stage of *"Fana"* or Annihilation — annihilation, not of what is Real (which is impossible), but of the false sense of separative existence. This teaching was also expressed by Lord Jesus, when he said *"If you would follow me, you must leave self behind."* The second part, or *"search for the lost 'self' in Existence,"'* corresponds to the stage of *"Baqa,"* or Subsistence — Life in God. Again, it is seen, as in so many spiritual traditions, the Sufi way is to negate the unreal. This is expressed as an unveiling, which reveals the Divine Beloved. The spiritual seeker or *dervish*, is the lover who longs for union with the Beloved. *"Ittihad"* is a Sufi technical term which means *"Union in the sense that things are non-existent, and their existence is God's."*

Christianity Teaches Discrimination

That there is such striking similarity regarding this idea in the Vedantic, Tantric, and Sufi traditions is hardly surprising, but it is certainly not limited to these; they are but several examples out of many. In the Christian tradition, as well, the two phases of spiritual discrimination are equally present. In the tradition of the Eastern Orthodox Christian Church, for example, the negative phase of spiritual discrimination is called *Apophatic theology.* The positive phase is *Cataphatic theology.* In Catholic parlance, they are, respectively, the "via negative" and the "via positive."

(1) The negative phase has been called the *"Dark Night of the Soul"* by St. John of the Cross, referring to that stage in which the soul is passing beyond the comfort of familiar, worldly reference points, as all which enables continued identity with the world is stripped away. The attitude that is recommended here, and also with great effect in the *Book of Job*, is that of calm resignation to the will of God. Corresponding to this, the Shakta, or Divine Mother worshiper [of Indian Tantra] lays bare his/her neck to the sword of the Goddess, taking all that comes from Her, be it pleasant or painful, as being for her/his own good.

(2) The positive phase can be seen in the Christian symbol of the "Ascent of Mount Carmel," which from another perspective, hints at the gradual ascent and awakening of Kundalini

Shakti — awakening into Divine Mother Reality. But more essentially in the Christian tradition, it is called "Resurrection." Again, this cannot truly be described, but merely surrendered to. For, it is the *"Peace that passes all understanding."*

Finally, Christ himself engaged in both these phases of spiritual discrimination when he negated the unreal, separative existence by his words, *"Of myself, I can do nothing,"* then affirmed God as the foundational or Ultimate Reality by saying, *"The Father within me does all these things."* When someone tried to attribute divinity to his individual, bodily form, he gently pointed out their misunderstanding, saying: *"Why do you call me good? There is only One who is good: Your Father who art in heaven."*

Judaism Teaches Discrimination

In Judaism as well, discrimination is an integral part of true spirituality. As in other religions, true spiritual discrimination is taught primarily within its deeper, esoteric tradition, called *Kabbalah*. The small gem of a book, *Open Secret*, by Rabbi Rami Shapiro, consists of letters written by a Jewish spiritual seeker to his Rebbe or Hassidic spiritual Master, and the Master's replies to his disciple, luminous with deep spiritual teachings and non-dual insight. In one passage, the Master teaches that God has two great aspects, which are *"Yesh"* or Being, and *"Ayin"* or Nonbeing. Discrimination between the two is the important implication which the student is led to understand. It is possible *"Ayin"* may be equivalent to the Eastern principle of *Maya*, or even the Buddhist designation of *"Anatman."*

Whatever the case may be, a conversation with a Hassidic Rabbi showed me conclusively that some sort of parallel does exist. I was invited by a Jewish friend to attend an open class being given by this teacher. Several in attendance were not Jewish, so in an effort to help us better understand Judaism, he said, "It is important to understand that in Judaism, this world is not considered to be real. It does not truly exist. Only God is real." When the class concluded, I thanked him and told him that in Hinduism, there is also the saying "The world is unreal; God alone is Real." He found that very interesting, yet he did not seem especially surprised.

Finally, there is this beautiful Kabbalistic teaching from Samuel L. Lewis, in his book *The Jerusalem Trilogy: The Song of the Prophets*. The Real is expressed by the Hebrew word *"Mi,"* meaning "who." The unreal is expressed by the word *"Ma,"* meaning "what." From the book, here are their definitions:

Mi: the life-force of creation; in man, the spirit or life-breath which vitalizes the body. In Jewish mysticism, this term corresponds to the Siva and Purusha of Hindu philosophy. 'It is the interaction between Siva and Shakti, between Mi and Ma, which accounts for all of life. (Glossary, p. 66)

Ma: The substance of creation; in man, the physical body as the accommodation of spirit or lifeforce. In Jewish mysticism, this term corresponds to the Shakti and Prakriti of Hindu philosophy. (Glossary, p. 65)

In chapter one he speaks of discrimination between these two: *"Who is Mi and what is Ma? Know this and perceive all things."* (Book I: the Day of the Lord Cometh, p. 43) Further on, he discriminates between the material elements and the Light of Being that is only reflected in them: *"And as the electron reveals the light in things, so am I the Light in the things of earth and spirit of man."*

One may also note that in the book of Genesis, God divided the heavens and the earth. The inner meaning here is that we are to do likewise, in the sense of understanding the one as real, and the other as illusory — the heavens symbolizing Spirit, the earth symbolizing matter. A further clue is given in the Christian New Testament, in which Saint Paul, who is understood to have studied the Jewish esoteric tradition, says: *"The first man was of the earth, made of dust; the second Man is the Lord from Heaven."* He is describing first the state of ignorance in which we are identified with matter, and then the liberated state which dawns once we have successfully discriminated and realized the Self within.

Buddhism Teaches Discrimination

In the Buddhist tradition, one of Lord Buddha's most important teachings was on the idea of "Anatman" or "No Self." Anatman does not mean that there is no First Principle, no primordial Ground of Being, whether we choose to call it *Brahman* or *Buddha Nature*. Rather, it means that all "compounded things" or objects which arise as the aggregate of relative conditions, cannot be the Self. In the sutras, the Buddha said: *"Bhikshus: there is only one authentic, undeceiving reality, and that is the reality of Nirvana. All composite things are deceptive and false."*

Even the small, individual self is a mistaken view arising from ignorance of the true nature of Being, which can never be divided. Sri Ramakrishna Paramahamsa likened such division to a line drawn on water which has only a temporal appearance. The Buddhist teaching of *Anatman* has its parallel in the yogic practice of *neti neti*. Wisely, this Buddhist mode of discrimination avoids the pitfall of trying to define the experience arising from the practice. Therefore, the negative phase of discrimination is especially emphasized. For, once the veils of illusory superimposition have been stripped away, what more is necessary? Knowledge of Buddha Nature spontaneously arises.

Tibetan teacher, Khenpo Tsultrim Gyamtso, writes on the precise nature of reality that a Buddha is one who knows that *"The appearances of phenomena arising, abiding, and ceasing are just mere appearances that have no inherent self nature."* Further, he states that *"Though it is the case that phenomena are of the nature of emptiness, it is important for us to be able to distinguish between the way of appearance and the way of Reality, because it is as a result of not knowing the way of Reality that we ordinary beings mistakenly think that appearances are real, and this is what causes all our problems."* (Sun of Wisdom: Teachings on the noble Nagarjuna's Fundamental Wisdom of the Middle Way, p. 84). Once again, discrimination is being stressed, and in a manner that is reminiscent of the deeper insights of the Vedanta philosophy. As Chandrakirti states in his text, *Entering the Middle Way*:

> There are two ways of seeing everything,
> The perfect way and the false way,
> So each and every thing that can ever be found
> Holds two natures within.

And what does perfect seeing see?
It sees the suchness of all things.
And false seeing sees what appears, no more.
This is what the perfect Buddha said.

From Age to Age it Renews

Spiritual discrimination is not limited to ancient traditions alone, but even finds expression in the modern, New Age revelation called, *A Course in Miracles*. And why should it be otherwise? Throughout the ages, human understanding of the truth of existence has always found fresh expression, to reconnect with each successive generation, each successive culture. At the beginning of *A Course in Miracles*, this principle of spiritual discrimination, in both of its phases, is succinctly expressed: *"Nothing Real can be threatened. Nothing unreal exists. Herein lies the peace of God."* Not surprisingly, this is said to sum up the entire "Course." This only makes sense, as discrimination is the basic foundation of spiritual practice and understanding. This verse from the "Course" is strongly reminiscent of the influence of India's realized souls and scriptures on the world, for, as Sri Krishna taught Arjuna on the battlefield of Kurukshetra: *"The unreal has no existence; the Real never ceases to be. The truth about both has been realized by the seers."* (Bhagavad Gita, II:16, trans. Swami Chidbhavananda)

How Does One Practice?

Although contrary to what some may believe, pure philosophical discrimination is not merely abstract theory; it is eminently practical. Still, one may wonder: "How can I put these ideas into real universal practice?" To answer this question, it is important to understand that working directly with the mind is the way to practice, for all delusion exists within the mind as a mistaken view of reality. So to correct this mistake, we must begin where the mistake begins, in the mind itself. Therefore, the pure practice is necessarily an abstract one. The alternative to this would be to take the concrete, the physical world, to be ultimately real. This is not a good alternative from the yogic standpoint, and is not sensible.

There are some helpful illustrative examples of the actual traditional practice *(neti neti)* in the excellent Nectar article "Adhara; The System of the Five Koshas" by Annapurna Sarada (Fall 2000 issue). Here, the author discriminates, step by step, between Brahman and each of the five Koshas — the temporary sheaths in which Consciousness manifests itself:

1. "I am not the body." (Annamayakosha)
2. "I am not the vital energy." (Pranamayakosha)
3. "I am not the mind." (Manomayakosha)
4. "I am not the intellect." (Vijnanamayakosha)
5. "I am not the sheath of bliss." (Anandamayakosha)

In each particular case, the attributes of the kosha under examination are extensively delineated using clear reason to show how unlike, and how dependent it is upon Brahman for its expression. And again, in each case, the inherent divine nature of the true Self, standing in stark contrast to the attributes of that illusory sheath, is reaffirmed.

For example, with respect to the body: *"The body is made of the combination of the five elements. It is subject to birth, disease and death and has qualities like fat and thin, young and old, attractive and unattractive. It depends on food and dies without it. Atman depends on nothing; It is self-existent. I see the body and its attributes, therefore they cannot be my Self. I cannot die, never having been born. Not bound by time, I have no age. Not bound by space, I have no specific location. I am the Atman, unchanging, ever pure and free from location. I am the Atman, unchanging, ever pure and free from modifications."*

And so on, in the case of each respective sheath, the writer discriminates in similar fashion [drawing from Shankara's Vivekachudamani – ed]. To extrapolate from the examples she has given in her article, we may each reason similarly with respect to the koshas, the tattvas, the elements, etc. In short, any and all manifest principles and the objects of gross or subtle sense experience are distinct from Divine Subject who is experiencing them.

Direct Self-Inquiry

Now that we have examined the two universal phases of spiritual discrimination in some detail, and also explored a concrete example of practical application of this idea, it is worth mentioning that there is an open space beyond all such movements of the mind which is the path of direct self-enquiry, called *Atma Vichara*. Engaging in Atma Vichara, the *jiva* or individuated Atman will know its identity with *Paramatman* or Infinite Being. Sri Ramana Maharshi was one shining exemplar of this path. Sri Ramakrishna was another, but he also advised negation of the unreal for beings who yet take this transient world to be real. For most of us, discrimination must still progress via negative and affirmative phases.

But in the path of direct enquiry as taught by Ramana, the seeker continually asks the question "Who am I?" — not so much with the intention of engaging logic or receiving a conceptual "answer," but more in line with allowing Reality to unfold knowledge of Itself, by Itself, and to Itself — without any limited or wishful projection or concealment on our part. In this way, one is not affirming or denying anything in the usual sense, but merely inquiring into Reality. The enquiry itself does not, except perhaps in the beginning stages, take the form of discursive thought, and neither does the "answer." The answer to this question is Truth, is Knowledge, is Consciousness.

One could go so far as to say that the answer to this question is revelation — not in the Western dualistic sense of that word, but in the same sense as *"drishya,"* or "seeing" one's identity (continuity) with one's own Substratum or "Ground of Being." As Jesus has said, *"My Father and I are one."* The *rishis* of ancient India were so-called (rishi having the same root as drishya/seer), because in deep, superconscious meditation, they "saw" the nondual Truth of their being. In sympathy with Jesus, they could also affirm, as he affirmed, *"I am the Way, the Truth, and the Life."*

The enlightened Sufi Mystic al-Hallaj, having matured in Self-knowledge via Islamic modes of discrimination, similarly proclaimed *"ana'l Haqq!"* or *"I am the Truth!"* And like Jesus, he was martyred by those who could not understand.

This direct Self-enquiry is silent, non-conceptual, and for those who understand, not even dependent upon words such as "Who Am I." The words "Who Am I" are only symbolic of the quality of attentiveness to Reality, which some Zen masters have called "bare attention." (Zen meditation is the embodied practice of that attentiveness). The Sufis speak of "Illumination by Presence" as a way beyond what the great Sufi Master Ibn Arabi termed, "The Confusion of the Philosophers." This Islamic "Presence Theology" also implies that very same direct, silent Self-enquiry.

Most of the time our minds are scattered (*vikshipta*), and their energies dispersed. In other words, we are not collected or "present." In this all too common state, which seers have called the "monkey mind," how can we possibly know Reality? But if we are truly attentive – as Lord Jesus says, *"If thine eye be single"* – our minds pointedly concentrated on Existence as It is rather than as we would like it to be, this Truth of Existence would be self-evident to us at all times. As Jesus said, *"Know the Truth, and the Truth shall set you free"* and *"Seek and you shall find."* Here, "seek" means the enquiry of *"attentiveness to what is,"* and *"you shall find"* means Gnosis, or Divine Knowledge. The Christian writer William H. Shannon, in his book, *Silence on Fire*, has termed this the "Prayer of Awareness." Lex Hixon, known also as Sheikh Nur al-Jerrahi, has called it "The Insomnia of Yoga."

Aspects of Discrimination Do Not Contradict

Does any of this mean that such direct enquiry supercedes the need for the traditional phases of discrimination, or that it is a new, unique understanding in relation to them? The answer is "no" on both points. The truth of the matter is that the experience of silent, Self-enquiry, is inherent in the traditional approaches of the East and the West, arising naturally as the process of discrimination matures. It is not new, but has been around as long as Enlightenment itself. It has not always been spoken of directly, for how does one put realization into words? The content of revelation is unadorned, naked Reality. As one spiritual writer has expressed in his unique translation of the Sanskrit phrase *"Om Tat Sat," "Om — That Inexpressible Reality!"*

But Sri Ramana Maharshi had the gift of being able to speak very openly and concisely on this subject, helping to clarify what has always been subtly implied in the traditional approaches. What he was able to elucidate was not the Reality Itself, for as we have seen, that is beyond what can be put into words, but he did very clearly outline and even formalize the practice and experience of *Atma Vichara*, which leads us directly to that knowledge. In his case, and that of Sri Ramakrishna, they knew their true natures; that Knowledge was inherent.

For most practitioners, however, and given our current spiritual capacity, it would not be practical to divorce traditional spiritual discrimination from subtle Self-enquiry. Is that even possible? For, in one sense, they are complementary. But it can also be said that they are the same; for discrimination between the Real and the unreal is not at all different from enquiry into the Self. The formal practice of discrimination will make us ready, and give us the capacity to enquire into the nature of the Self and to dwell in That, and keep us from falling back into delusion.

One Diamond, Many Facets

To conclude, spiritual discrimination is truly universal, seen in many spiritual paths and practices. It goes to show that Truth Itself is *Sanatana Dharma* — the Eternal Religion — whether the path that leads us to It is called Islam, Hinduism, Buddhism, Judaism, or Christianity. All the great religions contain some method for discrimination between the Real and the unreal in them. These are not merely intellectual correspondences, but lay out clearly the mystic way into the heart of Reality.

And this discrimination must be present in religion, for in its absence, mere belief replaces authentic realization. If one is willing to dig a little deeper, to look beneath the surface, it will be seen that while its cultural expression and practice may differ outwardly, the essential meaning is always the same. And its aim, which is always the same as its meaning, is always the Peace, the Joy, and the Freedom, that can only be fully known in God.

The Truth Shall Set You Free

It has been shown what spiritual discrimination is, how it is conceived of in various religious traditions, that its practice transcends differences of culture and creed, and that it qualifies one for the superlative knowledge of God. But once that realization dawns, how then shall we live? The answer comes down to us from an enlightened sage of ancient India:

"In the citadel of the body there is the small, sinless, and pure lotus of the heart which is the residence of the Supreme Being. In the interior of this tiny area is the sorrowless space of Light. That is to be meditated upon continually." Mahanarayana Upanisad

Paravasta has been a student of Vedanta and has studied with Babaji Bob Kindler since 1994. A serious practitioner of religion, he previously took hand in the Sufi Ruhaniat Order and also studied Essene Nazirite Christianity to become an ordained Essene minister.

Rabbi Rami Shapiro ◆

ADVAITIC JUDAISM
and the "Hindu Rabbi," Vivekananda

A note from the author reads: *"My goal here isn't to offer a definitive look at the parallels between Swami Vivekananda and Judaism, but only to make clear that Swamiji and Judaism have much to say to one another. I do this to honor the memory of my Hindu rabbi on the 150th anniversary of his birth, and as a catalyst to dialogue between Hindu and Jewish advaitists that we might continue the work of Swamiji by deepening our understanding of each other, each other's culture, and of the One who is all."*

Swami Vivekananda, like most Hindus of his day, may have known little about Judaism, and what he did know was probably filtered through the lens of Christianity. If this is true, he would have been pleasantly surprised, then, to know that Judaism has a rich Advaita tradition, and that many of his own teachings find resonance in Judaism as well. In this brief essay I seek to give you a glimpse of that resonance by offering a Jewish take on some of Swamiji's universal teachings set forth on the Ramakrishna Order's website, (www.ramakrishna.org).

Before I do, however, let me remind you that there is no such thing as "Judaism," just as there is no such thing as "Hinduism." Both traditions are too old, too dynamic, and too decentralized to lend themselves to a single school or vision. "Judaism" is a catch-all term for the varied and often conflicting opinions of Jewish sages over the millennia. What ties Jews together is a common library: a set of books and teachings we hold central to our culture and our spiritual lives. How we understand and use this library is up to each individual Jew. While I will rest my Judaism on the great lights of this library, never forget it is "my Judaism," and nothing more.

According to Swami Vivekananda, the heart of worship is to *"see God in all. This is the gist of all worship — to be pure and to do good to others."* While it is impossible to separate the nonduality of God from the moral stance of doing good to others, for sake of clarity let me do just that.

Rabbi Moshe Cordovero (1522-1570), one of the most famous and influential teachers of the Zohar, the "bible" of Jewish mysticism, explained the nonduality of God this way: *"God is found in all things and all things are found in God, and there is nothing devoid of divinity. Everything is in God, and God is in everything and beyond everything, and there is nothing beside God."* (Eilima Rabatti, Fol. 25a. Lvov, 1881).

Two centuries later, Rabbi Schneur Zalman of Liadi (1745-1812), the founder of Chabad Hasidism, wrote: *"Everything is God, blessed be He, who makes everything be, and in truth the world of seemingly separate entities is entirely annulled."* (Likkutei Torah, Shir haShiraim, fol. 41a)

When we speak of God we have to be careful not to imagine any thing in particular. In Judaism God is YHVH understood as Ehyeh asher Ehyeh, (Exodus 3:14). "I will be what I will be" and links this to the four letter name of God, YHVH. Despite English translations to the contrary, YHVH does not mean Lord, and Ehyeh asher Ehyeh doesn't mean "I am that I am." YHVH and Ehyeh are both forms of the Hebrew verb, hayah, to be. God is not a being or even a Supreme Being, but Being itself. God is a verb, not a noun or pronoun. As Rabbi Menachem Mendel Schneerson (1902-1994) put it: *"The absolute reality of God, while extending beyond the conceptual borders of 'existence,' also fills the entire expanse of existence as we know it. There is no space possible for any other existences or realities we may identify — the objects in our physical universe, the metaphysical truths we contemplate, our very selves — do not exist in their own reality; they exist only as an extension of divine energy."* (Toward a Meaningful Life, Simon Jacobson, ed. New York: William Morrow & Company, 1995, p. 215)

From the Advaita Jewish point of view, then, God isn't in all things, or outside all things: God is all things. Every encounter is a God encounter. This fits in well with Swamiji's teaching that one *"who sees Shiva in the poor, in the weak, and in the diseased, really worships Shiva. One who sees Shiva only in the image, his worship is but preliminary."* Jewishly, we would say, *"Love your neighbor as yourself"* (Leviticus 19:18), knowing that both neighbor and self are equal manifestations of the singular YHVH. And while much of priestly Judaism (as with priestly Hinduism) revolves around the Temple, the prophets, like Swami Vivekananda, saw this as "preliminary" at best. Here is but one example:

How shall I worship YHVH and honor the high God?
Shall I approach Him with burnt offerings and year-old calves?
Would YHVH be pleased with the sacrifice of a thousand rams?
How about the offering of ten thousand streams of oil?
Or is the sacrifice of my firstborn the price for my sins?
Of course not!
YHVH has told us, Humanity, what is required:
Do justly, act kindly, and walk humbly with your God.
(Micah 6: 6-8)

Judaism is about engaging life with justice and mercy, and holding our beliefs about God humbly, knowing, as the Rig Veda tells us, that *"Truth is one. Different people call it by different names."* Swami Vivekananda taught, *"One who has served and helped one poor person, seeing Shiva in him, without thinking of caste, creed, or race, or anything, with such a one Shiva is more pleased than with one who sees Him only in temples."* The rabbis of the Talmud would agree. They put it this way: *"One who sustains a single life is as one who sustains the entire world,"* (Talmud, Sanhedrin 37a).

The truest worship in both Swamiji's Hinduism and rabbinic Judaism is service to those in need. Swamiji taught, *"It is impossible to find God outside of ourselves. Our own souls contribute all of the divinity that is outside of us. We are the greatest temple. The objectification is only a faint imitation of what we see within ourselves."* Judaism shares a similar idea, but is not so keen on diminishing the outer dimension in favor of the inner. Listen to this teaching of Rabbi Levi Yitzchak of Berditchev (1740-1809):

> *Where can I find You, and where can I not find You?*
> *Above, only You; Below, only You;*
> *To the East, only You; To the West, only You;*
> *To the South, only You; To the North, only You;*
> *If it is good, it is You; If it is not, also You;*
> *It is You. It is only You.*

For us God is both inside and outside. The ancient rabbis called God HaMakom, "The Place," and meant by this that God is the place in which life arises; God is the source and substance of all being and becoming. From the perspective of God, "in" and "out" make no sense, and a temple is no more holy than a turd:

"The whole earth is filled with this [divine] presence; there is no place devoid of it. There is nothing besides the presence of God; being itself is derived from God and the presence of the Creator remains in each created thing." (Menachem Nahum of Chernobyl, Meor Einayim, Noah, trans. Arthur Green, *The Light of the Eyes*, p. 100)

Swami Vivekananda knew how hard it is for us to awaken to the reality of God. *"To succeed, you must have tremendous perseverance, tremendous will. 'I will drink the ocean,' says the persevering soul, 'at my will mountains will crumble up.' Have that sort of energy, that sort of will, work hard, and you will reach the goal."*

But the difficulty is not because God is far away, only because we fail to pay attention. *"Surely, this instruction that I enjoin upon you this day is not too baffling for you, nor is it beyond your reach. It isn't in the sky, that you should say, 'Who among us can fly up to the sky and get it for us and impart it to us, that we may live it?' Neither is it beyond the sea, that you should say, 'Who among us can cross to the other side of the sea and get it for us and impart it to us, that we may live it?' No, the thing is very close to you, in your mouth and in your heart, to live it."* (Deuteronomy 30:11-14)

Because we are so distracted from the truth, we imagine that whatever spiritual attainment is, it is reserved for the mighty few who can transcend the world to find it. Judaism doesn't ask us to transcend the world, but to embrace it and to engage all beings as manifestations of the one and only Being, God. When Swamiji tells us to *"stand up for God; let the world go,"* he isn't telling us to ignore the suffering of the world. Indeed we have just heard him tell us that caring for others is the superior form of worship. What he is saying is that we need to abandon any thought if imposing our will upon the world. Having complete trust in God is having complete trust in reality itself. And having such trust allows us to be vehicles for God's will rather than agents of self-will.

Rabbi Tarfon used to say, *"You are not expected to complete the task, but neither are you free to abandon it."* (Pirke Avot 2:21) The task is healing the world with justice and compassion, and the way to do this is to see self and other as manifestations of God. This is difficult because we insist we are apart from God rather than realizing we are a part of God. But God isn't far from us; God is us. We only have to realize who we are to know Who God is.

How are we do to this? Swamiji tells us: *"Giving up all other thoughts, with the whole mind day and night worship God. Thus being worshiped day and night, He reveals himself and makes His worshippers feel His presence."* Torah says something similar: *"Love YHVH your God with a whole heart, with every breath, and with all you have and are,"* (Deuteronomy 6:5) Remember, YHVH isn't a "God" somewhere in time or space, but the very is-ing and be-ing of reality. To love YHVH is to love life in all its forms. We do this, as Swami Vivekananda says, by giving up all other thoughts. But how are we do this? In Judaism, as in Hinduism, the practice is the continual recitation of God's Name.

As with Hinduism, Judaism, too, offers dozens of mantras. Some of these are actual Names of God, others, phrases from Torah, especially from Psalms. Personally, I recite HaRachaman, the Compassionate One. I have been doing this for almost twenty years, and while I make no claim to mastery, Judaism clearly states what this mastery is. Here is how the 18th century rabbi Dov Ber put it: *"A person would be so absorbed in this practice that there is no longer awareness of self. There is nothing but the flow of life; all thoughts are with God. One who still knows how intensely goes the practice has not yet overcome the bonds of [egoic] life."* (Or Ha-Emet, 2b)

Rabbi Rami Shapiro, PhD, is an author and professor of religious studies at Middle Tennessee State University. He was initiated into the Ramakrishna Order in the summer of 2009 by Swami Swahananda, who was initiated in 1937 by Swami Vijnanananda, one of Sri Ramakrishna's direct disciple.

Swami Aseshananda ◆

ON SWAMI VIVEKANANDA
Why Hundreds of Thousands now Adore Him

Transcribed from two lectures on Swami Vivekananda, given in 1986 and 1988, this discourse by the late Swami Aseshananda was delivered around the time of Swami Vivekananda's birthday on January 11th, 1988, in Portland Oregon, at the Vedanta Society of Portland. The SRV Associations, which Swami Aseshananda gave his personal blessing on in the early 1990's, is very gratified to be able to transcribe his lectures for publication in successive issues of Nectar of Nondual Truth, for as long as it exists to carry on the great work of Swami Vivekananda in the West and in the world.

We have assembled here to celebrate the birth anniversary of Swami Vivekananda who came to this country to represent Vedanta philosophy in 1893. The coming of Swami Vivekananda is an important event in the history of the world. That is because America has accepted two streams of thought. First, is Greek thought. Greek thought has given the American people a logical mind; you must be a man of reason, a man of sound judgement. Jefferson drafted the Declaration of Independence being prompted by the rational philosophers of Europe.

So here you find that the Greek mind is a logical mind. It wants precision. It also wants comprehension of the truth by the intellect. And that is the reason why when I hear the sacred song called *Kandana Bhava Bandana*, by Swami Vivekananda, it reminds me of Aryan thought; something "beyond." The Greeks had no concept of the beyond. They based all on the concept of this world in order to build a proud and civilized society which would dominate other societies — just like this affluent society called America. But an affluent society, if it does not produce an illumined soul, has no real meaning. If you cannot produce a single illumined soul in your American society, what power, what glory, what grandeur is contained in your rational civilization and your scientific achievement — and in creating a hydrogen bomb for the destruction of the world.

America has accepted another stream of thought. That thought is the Hebrew thought. That is God. And this God is in history. We must follow the commandments of God, and then God will give us happiness in this world and also bring contact with Him. Then, if you go to the place of worship, and follow his rules and regulations, you'll be able to live a happy life after death in paradise or in heaven.

Both these streams of thought think in terms of society, in terms of nation, in terms of culture, which must necessarily be intellectual — and which must be monotheistic. But Swami Vivekananda came as a representative of the rishis of the Upanisadic era. He did not preach monotheism, nor intellectualism, but Transcendentalism. And although Transcendentalism made a short visit to America, it did not live there because it did not follow the proper method of the ancient tradition. The Transcendentalism of Emerson and Thoreau had its origin from the East, from the Bhagavad Gita and the Upanishadic Truths. For example, there was Emerson's idea of Brahman, *"I am the doubter and the doubt."* But their Transcendentalism did not live; instead, pragmatism flourished, and it will flourish for a long time here.

But Swami Vivekananda is an adept awakener of the Consciousness of the American people, and of the western people. This is not just my statement; Mary Louise Burke also said so. She has made a statement that the hope of America is Swami Vivekananda. But in her works she concentrated only on his personality. Swami Vivekananda would not have liked that. The real hope of America, then, is what he brought here: Advaita. Swami Vivekananda is a representative of Advaita, nondualistic philosophy, which is the authentic strand running through the philosophy of Plato and Aristotle, and the underlying tenet in dualistic philosophy and the monotheism of Judeo/Christian faith.

Great Western Minds

Great minds have been watching the western countries for millennia. First, there is Saint Paul; second, is Saint Augustine; third, is Saint Thomas Aquinas. All these great minds have contributed to religion, but mostly to cultures which value prosperity and affluence most highly. They were high-minded, no doubt, but did not focus on the direct experience of God. For them it was more a matter of faith in God. Their doctrines, dogmas, creeds, and so forth were affected by the influence of Saint Paul, but it was he who brought in the erroneous idea of original sin. Saint Augustine proceeded only by faith. Regarding Thomas Aquinas, he wanted to build a bridge of understanding between reason and faith, about which he called the natural and the supernatural. But reason works in the field of nature, so his five proofs of the existence of God brought the Christians only an intellectual conviction. After that, if you want salvation, you have to accept Christ as the only savior, as the only redeemer. But how could Christ save those who lived prior to his advent? Reincarnation is not taught in the Bible.

About all of your problems, all of your doubts, all of your conflicts, all of your tensions, Swami Vivekananda is teaching a

> "He who wears the form must wear the chain." And what is Swamiji talking about in this line? Behind the name and form of every individual there is an Essence. And that Essence Swamiji calls Atman, or what you call Spirit in this country. Christ also called It that. God is a Spirit. They who worship God, worship his Spirit — and the Truth."

different way. He is affirming your Divinity. When Swamiji preached the philosophy of the Divinity of man, he did not think in terms of dualism, rather, he thought of Advaita. Your real nature is infinite. You have only hypnotized yourself into thinking that you are finite, that you are sinful, that you are born in sin and inequity. That is the reason why he said, *"Ye Divinities on earth, it is the greatest sin to call a man a sinner."*

So here, if you constantly harp on the depressing music of sin you will be a bundle of negativities, of emotions — of doubts, conflicts, and tensions. Therefore, the real "good news" for the American people is Swamiji's affirmation that mankind is Divine. That is, you are potentially Divine, but you must make this fact a matter of your experience. Recently, I got a Christmas card on which the Vedic words were written, *"From dreams awake, from bonds be free! Know the Truth that thou art He."* By the words "Thou art He" is meant Thou art Infinite. So, because Americans all like freedom; freedom is in the atmosphere.

Vivekananda Teaches True Freedom

They say that when a western boy or girl reaches the age of sixteen or so, they tell their mothers, "I want to be free." By this they mean "I want to get an apartment; I want to experience the world." The mother says, "No darling, you stay home. I will miss you and I'm so fond of you that I'll be heartbroken if you leave me." But what can the child do? The mind says that I want to be free.

This freedom is only a small step. It is governed by the laws of the parents. True freedom cannot be connected with law — neither the written law, called commandments, or laws of nature. The Greeks accepted the law of nature, while Mose's law is the written word called the ten commandments. But the Eastern idea is as long as you are bound by law you are not free. *"He who wears the form must wear the chain."* And what is Swamiji talking about in this line? Behind the name and form of every individual there is an Essence. And that Essence Swamiji calls Atman, or what you call Spirit in this country. Christ also called It that. God is a Spirit, they who worship God, worship his Spirit — and the Truth.

That is also the direction Swamiji took his lecture called "Christ the Messenger." Jesus realized, he accepted, and he preached. That I am a disembodied, unfettered, Spirit, he said, so art thou also That. To all his disciples he preached, *"I and my Father are One."*

But Greeks will say that this is a speculative idea, a concept of the mind. But it is not to the likes of Swami Vivekananda and Shankaracharya; they experienced samadhi. So unfortunately, this precious stream of Advaita got completely lost in the western religious tradition over time. Advaita did visit in the form of Gnosticism, but Christian faith did not allow it to thrive. Then it came in the form Neo-Platinism, and it came by the influence of Meister Eckhart. But Meister Ekhart was not a guru, and there was no advaitic tradition that preceded him. With no authority, he was nearly excommunicated for introducing it.

Vedanta Today, and My Path

Today, at this time we will see what happens to America, as well as in the future. But on Swamiji's birthday, today, I can say that America has accepted Swamiji's message to some extent. There is an acceptance of monastic life, for instance. At this time there are twelve Vedanta centers, and two of them have convents as well. Further, every center encourages American boys and girls to live a life of renunciation in order to realize God, and to be a blessing to mankind.

On Swamiji's birthday, in the year 1921, 67 years ago, I went to join the monastery. I went just to be a worker. If I had gone as a guest, then they might have gotten tired of me, so I said, "Let me do some little work." I was engaged with the feeding of the poor. Swamiji's birthday there is called *Daridra Narayana,* and every man that comes is seen as a representative of God. I came as a guest, but it is Swamiji's blessing that made me stay. Swamiji has not failed me in all these years.

And then there was great difficulty in coming to America. At first I attended on Swami Nikhilananda in New York, who was a brilliant speaker. I had never learned how to give a speech, although I spoke once or twice in Bengali, but not in English. So then came the idea; either swim or sink. Self-preservation is the law of nature; nobody wants to be defeated. Life is a challenge. There were many obstacles, many difficulties, but I was patient.

Any kind of power must come from within. Therefore, I went to Holy Mother. You ask, "How did you go to Holy Mother, who had already passed?" Through meditation, and the mantra that She had given. It has tremendous power. Death is bound to come to every person, but one can become deathless by repeating the mantra which will awaken spiritual consciousness and finally lead to the goal. The goal is *Atmajnana,* knowledge of the true Self — which is not finite, but infinite; which is not limited, but unlimited; which is not changeful, but changeless; which is not created, but acreate.

I also studied Christianity at St. Paul's Cathedral Mission College. I found that the greatest force in the field of western theological religion is Paul. He was a short man, bent, a little this and that. He was not physically beautiful, but he had tremendous energy and enthusiasm. It is Paul who has formulated what is called the doctrine of Original Sin, and also the doctrine of Avatar as a Redeemer, as Savior.

But Avatar on the Eastern horizon is not a Redeemer, and not a Savior. Avatar is an exemplar. And that is why Swamiji, who early on had doubt about the existence of God, asked the question of everyone, "Have you seen God?" It was only Sri Ramakrishna who gave the categorical reply, *"Yes, I have seen Him in samadhi. You must also go into samadhi to find Him. If you go into Savikalpa Samadhi you will realize the personal God; you'll be the wave and God will be the Ocean. But if you go into Nirvikalpa Samadhi there is no distinction between you and God; pratyagatman and paramatman are identical."*

Advaita is Strength

In this country Swamiji preached Advaita. You will find plenty of dualism here, and an accent on the personal God, but he said that these eventually make a person weak. He felt that everything that makes a person strong should be accepted. You see, India, where he came from, is a place where Avatars flourish; they flourish like mushrooms [all laugh]. Now, in early days, there was one Jiten Thakur in Benares. We heard that he is was an Avatar, like Sri Ramakrishna. He talked to Divine Mother. He was a worshipper of Divine Mother, the Divine Mother supposedly incarnated once again.

One day, in the morning, this Jiten Thakur came with his disciples. An Avatar, you see, cannot come alone; he will have to have some disciples with him, as the sun will have its satellites. So, early morning, maybe 9-9:30, I went to see Swami Saradananda. He was meditating, absorbed in deep meditation, like Siva. Sometimes the japa beads would fall from his hand. He was not conscious of it; he was absolutely unconcerned and intensely absorbed in the experience of the Spirit. Afterwards I learned by seeing his diary, Communion with the Divine Mother, that "You are in me and I am in You."

Swami Saradananda, at first, did not want to come with me to see this new Thakur. "Ask him to come in the evening when I give audience with visitors" he said. I replied, "But he has brought lots of disciples, and they will be disappointed." So swami agreed to see them all. This Thakur arrived showing signs of bhava. Now, when you say "bhava" in this country, it may be related to the Quakers, you understand? Quakers were previously called "Shakers," as they also use to shake. So this Thakur was not only quaking, but shaking [all laugh]. He was shaking as if he were in ecstasy or rapture — in an exalted state of consciousness. Now Swamiji, a great yoga psychologist, would have said that it was nervous weakness, and that the man should take nutritious food [laughter] and see a good doctor in order to make the nerves strong.

Swami Saradananda had learned well from Swamiji. The point revolved around whether this Thakur's show was authentic spiritual experience. As soon as Swami Saradananda entered the room and saw the spectacle that was going on, and saw this Thakur coming forward to embrace him, he said strongly, "Stop that! Stop that!" Everyone became quiet. Swami Saradananda sat down, and this Thakur said, "Why not ask some questions of the swami?" But his disciples remained silent. Then Swami Saradananda felt a stirring and he asked the attendant to bring prasad. And prasad was brought. Then this Thakur said, "I will eat from the hand of "Sarada." Then Swami Saradananda, like a mother, fed him. That was the end of all the fuss.

This was real strength, not shaking and posturing from weakness, from desire for show and pretense. Strength is necessary. The westerners have also got strength, I understand — your atomic energy will give you strength, but it is also creating moral decline and decay. You must watch out! You have accepted the bhoga marg, the path of enjoyment based in domination over others. From cradle to the grave you teach your children have "fun." This will spell disaster. Only by self-control will you remain strong, will you remain invincible. All human civilizations who have achieved tremendous success have also collapsed in the heyday of their prosperity. Your hydrogen bomb will not give you strength. Your society will not give you strength. Your strength will come when you follow Sri Ramakrishna, when you follow the message of Swami Vivekananda. What is the message of Swami Vivekananda? Renunciation.

Renunciation, Purification, and an Illumined Soul

Renunciation, renunciation, renunciation. That is the true song, as I said. You should be soft, your beat should not be predominant. Here in the West, you see, people are clanging the cymbal and the beating the drum. The voice, the words, are never heard. That will not work. You should be subdued. The cymbal should be subdued. The voice should be strong. This was Swami Vivekananda; his demeanor was nonviolent, but his voice, and the Truth he spoke, were pronounced.

So, we adore him because he has broken the fetters of maya. And like a lion he has come out of the cage — the cage of time, space, and causation. But you are caught in that cage. Intellectualism will never help you. To come out of the cage of maya, of time, space, and causation, you have to purify your subconscious mind. The subconscious mind is purified when you come in contact with an illumined teacher. Just to see him, all samskaras, not only some of the samskaras, will become sattvic. In Indian tradition, then, in order to purify the mind a person will either go to the Ganges or go to an Illumined Soul.

To live with Swami Saradananda, who had been trained by Ramakrishna, Holy Mother, and Swamiji, was a great opportunity. After I got trained by him, I came as a guest to this country, but due to the grace of Swami Vivekananda he has allowed me to stay. And when I came to this country he knew the difficulty. You see, I was the representative of a "foreign religion," and India was under British rule. The West will only judge a nation by its society. If it is an affluent society, they will accept it. America appreciates Japan. Why? Because there are skyscrapers. Not only skyscrapers, there are automobiles and swimming pools and what not [laughter]. All things, all facilities are available in Tokyo, so they will go to Tokyo, not to a country where poverty, ignorance, and superstition have descended. But I must say that if anybody goes to India as a tourist, he will not understand. To know the heart of India one has to see great Souls like Sri Ramakrishna, Holy Mother, and Swamiji. A country that can produce a man like Ramakrishna and woman like Holy Mother is verily a priceless treasure of modern man.

When I think of Swami Vivekananda, I think of Sri Shankaracharya resisting the Buddhistic onslaught during its decline. The whole country was flooded by fallen Buddhistic ideas. Sometimes those ideas are nihilistic ideas. And it is Shankaracharya, a single man who resisted. Similarly, the western civilization, as it were, came like a flood to India when our religion was dead. It was Swami Vivekananda who resurrected that religion by coming in contact with Sri Ramakrishna. At first, Swamiji did not accept the concept of guru or the concept of image worship or the concept of Avatar. Swamiji first enlisted in or joined the Brahmo Samaj. Brahmo Samaj in India at the time is something like the Unitarian movement here today. The Brahmo Samaj movement is a movement who thinks in terms of social reform, and also thinks that intellectual understanding will solve the problems of life. But after coming in contact with Sri Ramakrishna his ideas underwent a tremendous change. He become the chief representative of the Master's message. And that message involves monastic life. Without monastic life, religion will not produce illumined Souls. Even householders will learn from the monks when they live a pure, stainless, and unadulterated life. That is called *brahmacharya*. That is the reason why brahmacharya, continence, is important for all.

The Role of Purity

In the book, *Reminiscences of Swami Vivekananda,* one of the disciples asked Swamiji about the secret to his success. "What is the source you have extracted so much power from?" And then he learned about his unbroken brahmacharya. That is why Swami Ramakrishnananda wrote several letters, published in Vedanta Kesari, to Swami Paramananda. He wrote, "Always remember unbroken brahmacharya if you want to represent Ramakrishna." Desiring enlightenment, man and woman should practice brahmacharya. The ideal woman is represented by Holy Mother. What is that ideal? Eternal virginhood. Similarly, the ideal man, Sri Ramakrishna, although he was married, is based in unbroken brahmacharya. That alone will give *Atmajnana*. Shankaracharya lived that life. Swami Vivekananda lived that life. And that is the reason why the Ramakrishna Order emphasizes it.

Swami Damodarananda from Fiji, he used to come here. At one time he was going to see Ramana Maharshi. I saw and met him in Ramana Maharshi's ashram. He was nice to me and all that. He said, "I see there are a bunch of ladies here. How will you be able to keep your mind calm?" I didn't reply. He said, "You need an atmosphere in which you can learn. Then he went to Bangalore. When he was in Madras he used to come to visit me, and we used to talk. But he was not inspired by talk, but by action. he had very good samskaras. Swami Tyagisananda was the head in Bangalore at that time. About Swami Damodarananda, then a young Brahmin boy, He told me, "I don't know this boy. He mentioned your name. What do you think of him?" I replied, "I don't know a hundred percent of this boy either, I have only talked with him. But why not give him a chance? We do not know. We are not omniscient. Thakur was omniscient; he could see. He could see all on one's face." Then Swami Tyagisananda gave him a chance, and he asked to see Tyagisananda. Tyagisananda was an ideal sadhu, a good sadhu; very scholarly, very noble, very austere. But he worked himself to death at the same time. Suppose you drive your car and you do not put gas in. Will the car go by itself? You may have a Mercedes or Rolls Royce or any other car, but it cannot move without gasoline. Similarly, Swami Tyagisananda was an ideal sadhu, but he worked too hard. A sadhu alone makes a sadhu, because Light brings Light. Swami Prabudhananda associated with Swami Tyagisananda, and then Swami Yatiswarananda.

I am most grateful to Swami Vivekananda. During his time, Bengal was flooded with emotionalism. Two races are very emotional: one is the French people; and Bengalis are also very emotional. That is because Bengal is flooded with Chaitanya followers; they are a bhakti movement. Similarly, the West is also flooded with a kind of bhakti, and emotionalism. Therefore, if the West does not accept *jnana marga*, it will be very difficult for the West to keep calm and balanced when the trials and tribulations of life assail it. As I have said, life is a challenge. How can we master challenge? Through dharma, through righteous living. What do we mean by righteous living? Not sense bound mind, but sense free mind. You see, very few people will think in terms of enlightenment, *jivanmukti*, but hundreds of people will think in terms of wealth, power, position, glory, honor, success, and acceptance of the vanities of this external world.

An Authentic Patriotism

So, Swamiji appealed to me because of his patriotism; that I will say. But after joining the monastery, patriotism is a lower ideal. That is the reason Swamiji said to Nivedita, *"Your nationalism, your patriotism, is a sin."* It creates an obstacle. A religious man should be universal. He does not belong to any country, any race, or any culture. And that is the reason, I tell you, that the other day I found that my passport has expired. I thought, "What am I going to do?" [laughter]. Then I thought, "This is a good thing. I do not belong to America, nor do I belong to India. Then to whom do I belong? To Sri Ramakrishna. What do I mean by Sri Ramakrishna? Universal Spirit — Ramakrishna represents the Universal Spirit. Ramakrishna represents

> "How can we master challenge? Through dharma, through righteous living. What do we mean by righteous living? Not sense bound mind, but sense free mind. You see, very few people will think in terms of enlightenment, *jivanmukti*, but hundreds of people will think in terms of wealth, power, position, glory, honor, success, and acceptance of the vanities of this external world."

Advaita. Ramakrishna represents *Atmajnana*. Ramakrishna means to explain *Jivanmukti*. Ramakrishna embodies "the peace that passeth all understanding"; Ramakrishna means *Nirvikalpa Samadhi*.

Mother Worship and the Genderless Atman

We find, then, that Swamiji's great gift is the bridge of understanding he forged between the East and the West. He came here without any credentials. He went to Chicago and found the Hale sisters. Swamiji used to say, "Mother Church, Father Pope, and the Hale sisters" [all laugh]. Many letters have been written by him, especially to Mary Hale. Swamiji told her that this world is maya, and if you can renounce you will find real happiness. There is no happiness in the world unless you go within. Dive deep into your own consciousness. The kingdom of heaven is within.

Swami Vivekananda started his work here with only two centers — in New York and in San Francisco. Now, other centers have come. You will find at each center that there are some brahmacharis and some are sannyasins. Why did they not go to a Catholic monastery? You see, Swamiji used to say that a true leader of religion will be a person who will have the brilliant intellect of a Shankara and the all-encompassing love of a Buddha. But Shankara did not allow women to join the monastic life; but Buddha allowed. And so Swamiji had this dream that there will be parallel organizations. As we have got the Ramakrishna Order, similarly, there should be the Sarada Order or Ramakrishna-Sarada Order. So, at the centenary time of Holy Mother, that Order started. Bharatiprana, who served Holy Mother, became the president. Bharatiprana use to give initiation, brahmacharya, and sannyas as our president does at the Belur Math.

So, this is the great idea, but not in the West. The Catholic order will not do it; every conservative Christian will not do it either. Women are of secondary importance because there is no concept of the genderless Atman here, only the concept of man and woman. This is nonsense. The idea of man and woman comes due to ignorance. If you are enlightened, there is no distinction between man and woman. Man must transcend his manhood, woman must transcend her womanhood, and both must realize their infinite nature — which is genderless as well as causeless. But that will not happen here. The West will not accept this ideal because of the teaching in the Book of Genesis — "God created man in his image." They take it literally, as with everything else in the Bible. But as long as one thinks in terms of creation and causation, so long will one think of their immortality.

No "Your Truth" or "My Truth:" Just, The Truth

The other day, Mr. Bush, lecturing, was talking about the Christian theologians all saying, "each in their own way." But it is not in the way that Gaudapada would interpret it, or Shankara would interpret it — nor Swami Vivekananda. The moment you accept birth to be real, then your death becomes real, and going to heaven or hell becomes real, and all such superstition. You will then never be able to accept your immortal nature. You can accept immortality only on the basis that you are unborn; that your real nature is deathless and that you do not have to go to heaven. You realize your true nature to be infinite existence, infinite knowledge, and infinite bliss. And that realization comes if you have a guru who is illumined, and who trains you in *Atmajnan*, and you become a true follower of the method through which you reach samadhi, nirvikalpa samadhi.

May we all reach that highest of all Goals, regardless of race, gender, class, or creed. May Love betide all; may Peace come unto all. May all see the face of Truth, and be fortified by the armor of Love.

> "Women are of secondary importance because there is no concept of the genderless Atman here, only the concept of man and woman. This is nonsense. The idea of man and woman comes due to ignorance. If you are enlightened, there is no distinction between man and woman."

Swami Aseshananda, a direct disciple of Sri Sarada Devi, Sri Ramakrishna's wife and spiritual consort, was the Spiritual Minister of the Vedanta Society of Portland for over forty years. He also received holy company with some of the direct disciples of the Great Master. He is the author of Glimpses of a Great Soul, on the life and teachings of Swami Saradananda.

SRV Associations — Babaji's Teaching Schedule, 2013

SRV Hawai'i
Administrative Office
PO Box 1364
Honoka'a, HI 96727

SRV Associations'
website: www.srv.org
email: srvinfo@srv.org
Phone: 808-990-3354

SRV Oregon
1922 SE 42nd Ave.,
Portland, OR 97215
Ph: 503-774-2410

SRV San Francisco
465 Brussels Street
San Francisco, CA 94134
Ph: 415-468-4680

February/March, 2013

SRV San Francisco (Meditation, 6 to 7 am)

2/6	Wed	7:00pm	Arati/Satsang
2/7	Thur	7:00pm	Arati/Satsang
2/8	Fri	7:00pm	Arati/Satsang
2/9	Sat	9:30am	Class: Svetasvataropanisad
		3:00pm	Children's Class
		7:00pm	**Brahmananda/Vivekananda Puja**
2/10	Sun	9:30am	Class: Svetasvataropanisad

Swami Vivekananda's 150th Birth Centenary Retreat
Seattle, WA – Feb 14 to 18
(arrive Thursday evening, depart Monday at noon)
For more information call SRV Office, 808-990-3354

SRV Oregon (Call for meditation times)
2/14-18 - Swami Vivekananda Retreat - Seattle

2/23	Sat	9:30am	Class: Svetasvataropanisad
2/23		6:00pm	SRV Puja, Siva Puja
2/24	Sun	9:30am	Class: Svetasvataropanisad
2/27	Wed	7:00pm	Scripture Class with Anurag
3/1	Fri	7:00pm	Arati/Satsang with Babaji
3/2	Sat	9:30am	Class: Svetasvataropanisad
3/2		6:00pm	SRV Puja, Siva Puja
3/3	Sun	9:30am	Class: Svetasvataropanisad

May, 2013

SRV San Francisco (Meditation, 6 to 7 am)

5/8	Wed	7:00pm	Arati/Satsang
5/9	Thu	7:00pm	Arati/Satsang
5/10	Fri	7:00pm	Arati/Satsang
5/11	Sat	9:30am	Class: Shankara & the Upanisads
		3:00pm	Children's Class
		7:00pm	SRV Puja
5/12	Sun	9:30am	Class: Divine Mother's Day

SRV Oregon (Call for meditation times)

5/17	Fri	7:00pm	Arati/Satsang with Babaji
5/18	Sat	9:30am	Class: Shankara & the Upanisads
		6:00pm	SRV Puja, Siva Puja
5/19	Sun	9:30am	Class: Upanisads

5/23-27 - Buddhism and Vedanta Retreat

Memorial Day Retreat — Buddhism and Vedanta
May 23rd through the 27th — Location TBA
(arrive Thursday evening, depart Monday at noon)

5/29 Wed 7:00pm Scripture Class with Anurag

6/1	Sat	9:30am	Class: Upanisads
		6:00pm	SRV Puja, Siva Puja
6/2	Sun	9:30am	Class: Upanisads

July/August, 2013

SRV San Francisco (Meditation, 6 to 7 am)

7/13	Sat	9:30am	Class: Upanisads
		3:00pm	Children's Class
		7:00pm	SRV Puja
7/14	Sun	9:30am	Class: Upanisads

SRV American River Retreat over Gurupurnima
July 17th through July 23rd

SRV Oregon (Call for meditation times)

7/27	Sat	9:30am	Class: Upanisads
		6:00pm	SRV Puja, Siva Puja
7/28	Sun	9:30am	Class: Upanisads
7/31	Wed	7:00pm	Scripture Class with Anurag

8/2-4 SRV 3-day Weekend Seminar — Mantra Tapas
(Mantra Teachings and Group Japa Practice)

October/November, 2013

SRV San Francisco (Meditation, 6 to 7 am)

10/2	Wed	7:00pm	Arati/Satsang
10/3	Thu	7:00pm	Arati/Satsang
10/4	Fri	7:00pm	Arati/Satsang
10/5	Sat	9:30am	Class: Srimad Devi Bhagavatam
		3:00pm	Children's Class
		7:00pm	**Durga Puja**
10/6	Sun	9:30am	Class: Srimad Devi Bhagavatam

SRV Kali Durga Navaratri Retreat
Buckhorn Springs, Ashland, OR – October 11th - 14th
In Celebration of SRV's 20th Anniversary

SRV Oregon (Call for meditation times)

10/19	Sat	9:30am	Class: Srimad Devi Bhagavatam
		6:00pm	**Durga Puja**
10/20	Sun	9:30am	Class: Srimad Devi Bhagavatam
10/23	Wed	7:00pm	Scripture Class with Anurag
10/25	Fri	7:00pm	Arati/Satsang with Babaji
10/26	Sat	9:30am	Class: Upanisads
		6:00pm	SRV Puja, Siva Puja
10/27	Sun	9:30pm	Class: Upanisads

---

* Vedanta for Teens & Children
at SRV Oregon and SRV San Francisco
Contact Annapurna Sarada — Ph: 808-990-3354

SRV Associations —
Babaji's Teaching Schedule, 2013
SRV Hawaii Ashram, Big Island

Sunday Classes, 2:30 - 5:30pm
Directions: Call: 808-990-3354

Jan 27 & Feb 3, 2013
Devotion of Nonseparation

March 17, 24, 31 & April 7, 14, 21, 28
Advaita of the Avatars

June 16, 23, 30 & July 7
Vedanta & Buddhism

August 18, 25 & Sept. 1, 8, 15, 22
Gaudapada's Non-Touch Yoga

November 10, 17, 24 & Dec. 1, 8, 15, 22
Shakta-Advaita-Vada

Notice:
This yearly schedule is subject to change.
Please check the calendar on our website
www.srv.org
and sign our e-list at classes for notifications
or read our e-newsletter, Mundamala.
You can also contact your local SRV center:
Hawaii & Oregon: 808-990-3354;
San Francisco: 415-468-4680

Check www.srv.org for Hawaii retreats
or see our Retreats Pages in this issue

Sign up for:
- SRV Magazine: Nectar of Non-Dual Truth
- Raja Yoga email study with Babaji
- SRV's Facebook page
- SRV's YouTube channel: Teaching videos
- Godblogs: Inspired Dialog

* Please call or inquire about our Children's Classes
Contact Annapurna Sarada — Phone 808-990-3354

SRV Hawai'i Administrative Office:	SRV Associations' website:
PO Box 1364	www.srv.org
Honoka'a, HI 96727	email:
Ph: 808-990-3354	srvinfo@srv.org

Join the SRV Facebook Group. Contact jamiji@gmail.com

SRV Bulletin Board

SRV Hawaii and Oregon Ashrams
SRV Associations maintains an ashram in Portland, Oregon and on the Big Island of Hawaii that rent out rooms to spiritual aspirants. This is an ideal opportunity to experience an extended retreat in a holy atmosphere. Contact us if you would like to interview for the next available opening.

Schools for Struggling Souls — Meeting the Need
SRV Associations currently teaches at five prisons in Oregon. We also provide books, magazines, and teaching handouts to inmates in Oregon and other states. This service has been increasing steadily over the last several years but our funding has not kept pace with the hundreds of miles we now travel and the increasing requests for spiritual reading material. Please consider donating to this very important cause. It is up to all of us to re-envision prisons as "schools for struggling souls" and provide for them as such. Donate online at www.srv.org or send your tax-deductible donation to:
SRV Associations, PO Box 1364,
Honoka'a, HI 96727
Ph. 808-990-3354

Nectar is Seeking Writers!
We need writers from all traditions, and especially the Abrahamic religions: Jewish, Christian, and Muslim/Sufi. Also writers representing Native traditions, Quaker, Zoroastrianism, and others. If you are a practitioner or teacher of one of these traditions, or know of one, please contact us for submission guidelines:
srvinfo@srv.org or 808-990-3354

SRV Associations — Retreats for 2013

Swami Vivekananda's 150th Birth Anniversary Retreat
February 14 – 18, 2013, Seattle, Washington

In 2013, millions of devotees, students, and admirers around the world will celebrate the birth of Swami Vivekananda who injected the liberating wisdom of Advaita Vedanta into western society at the turn of the last century. SRV students will have an opportunity to honor the great Swami by delving deeply into the message and teachings he delivered that altered the course of thinking humanity. Join Babaji Bob Kindler as he presents many profound aspects of Vivekananda: The great soul that Sri Ramakrishna brought for the good of the world, who sat at his feet as a young man; the World Teacher dispensing the knowledge of absolute Unity; and as Guru, brother-disciple, and friend to those who knew him.

"It is only the great saint who can work, making a mountain out of an atom of virtue in others and cherishing no desire but that of the good of the world." – Swami Vivekananda

"Swami Vivekananda, the epitome of spiritual authenticity, was the incarnation of Lord Siva in this age and a fully manifested Buddha living right in our own time and proximity." – Babaji Bob Kindler

Text: *Swami Vivekananda Vijnanagita*
Location: Seattle
Arrival: Thursday, February 14, after dinner and by 10:00pm
Departure: Monday, February 18, 12:00pm (approximately)
Tuition (all inclusive): $350 Registration: Starts now. Tuition is due by Feb 1
Financial hardship? Call 808-990-3354 to discuss options
Register by email: srvinfo@srv.org or by phone 808-990-3354

Buddhism & Vedanta
May 23 – 27, 2013, Wind River region, Washington

Babaji Bob Kindler, who holds a dual spiritual heritage via initiation into the Ramakrishna Lineage and Kagyu Tibetan Buddhism, will present essential and practical teachings from both systems. Babaji includes Lord Buddha's teachings as part of a comprehensive understanding of Advaitic non-dual Wisdom, and the Yogic pathways to Freedom that Mother India supplies in abundance.

This retreat is our first to take place on the sprawling properties of Windwood Waters. The main lodge where classes will be held is situated in the forest above the Wind River in the Columbia Gorge. The lodge has been remodeled from its earlier homestead days – natural wood beams and columns, plentiful windows, and the sunken fireplace area all make for a unique, rustic setting – a perfect modern forest ashram for our time in holy company.

Location: Near Stevenson, WA, directions given out before retreat
Arrival: Thursday, May 23, after 3:00pm and by 6:00pm dinner
Departure: Monday, May 27, 1:00pm
Registration: Starts now. Tuition and lodging fees are due by May 9th
Register by email: srvinfo@srv.org or by phone 808-990-3354
Costs: Tuition and meals: $375
Lodging: private room single, $240; private room shared with 1 - 2 others, $160/person;
semi-private lodge sleeping, $120*; Tenting, $80*
*bring your own bedding

SRV American River Retreat over Gurupurnima
July 17 – 23, 2013, Forest Hill, CA

- Live in holy company for a full week – meditating, studying, serving, and growing together.
- Each morning begins with chanting from the Bhagavad Gita prior to meditation.
- Daily classes include essential teachings of Yoga and Vedanta,
- Afternoons include explorations and swimming/sunning along the River
- Afternoon Chela Dharma class for teens and young adults
- Evening devotions at the altar, singing and chanting, meditation, and satsang.
- <u>Concurrent Children's Retreat</u> — Children, ages 6 to approximately 13 have their own simultaneous retreat. Activities include "salute to the sun," morning ritual, meditation, Vedic stories and lessons, and arts and crafts.

Location: Private land in Foresthill, California near the American River
Arrival: Arrive after 4pm, Wed, July 17
Last day of retreat: Tuesday, July 23 (approximately noon, clean up follows)
Tuition: all inclusive
 Adults: $600 (full retreat) $250 (weekend, arrive Friday) $100/day
 Children/Students: $270 (full retreat) $135 (weekend, arrive Friday) $45/day
Registration: starts now and tuition is due by Monday, July 1
Financial hardship? Call 808-990-3354 to discuss options
Register by email: srvinfo@srv.org or by phone 808-990-3354

Kali Durga Navaratri Retreat
October 10 – 14, 2013, Buckhorn Springs, near Ashland, OR
In celebration of SRV's 20th Anniversary

For SRV Association's third retreat on Mother Kali at Buckhorn Springs, the tradition continues with esoteric Tantric teachings, the presentation of Kali Sangeet (bhajans) and fresh wisdom charts for viewing. Perfect for initiates and lovers of Mother Reality, transformation in Kali's own atmosphere is the result.

Location: Buckhorn Springs, near Ashland, OR
Arrival: Thursday, October 10 after 4:00pm
Departure: Monday, October 14, 12:00pm (approximately)
Lodging/Meals: $435 dbl occupancy; $552 single **Tuition:** $345
Financial hardship? Call 808-990-3354 to discuss options
Registration: Starts now. Tuition and other fees are due by September 20, 2013
Register by email: srvinfo@srv.org or by phone 808-990-3354

Plus: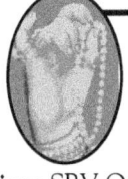

Mantra Tapas: 3-Day Weekend Seminar
August 2 – 4, 2013, SRV Oregon Ashram
Teachings on Mantra with Group Japa Practice

Location: SRV Oregon Ashram in Portland
Friday, Aug 2: 6:00am – 5:00pm (breakfast/lunch)
Saturday, February 11: 6:00am – 8:00pm (3 meals served)
Sunday, February 12: 6:00am – 5:00pm (breakfast/lunch)

Tuition: $295, (all-inclusive) Due by Sunday, Feb 5
Accommodations: This is a non-residential seminar
Contact us if you would like assistance with lodging.
 808-990-3354 // srvinfo@srv.org

During this weekend seminar, Babaji will present the multileveled facets of mantra and its practice.
As Sri Ramakrishna has stated, "It takes only a tiny germ to kill an elephant."
The mantra is the germ that kills the elephant of ignorance, ego, distraction, karma, negativity, and more.

Advaita-satya-amritam

NECTAR
of Non-Dual Truth

Donation/Order Form
Suggested donation $7 per issue

*Nectar is available for free if you write, email, or call for a copy.
Your generous donations make Nectar available to others and help us to widen our distribution.*

Those who donate $7 or more for the next issue, will be added to our subscriber's list.
- ❏ Please send me/my friend a free copy of the next issue of Nectar.
- ❏ Send me ___ copies to give to friends or a spiritual center of my choice.
- ❏ I am enclosing the names of persons/centers I want to receive Nectar. *Fill out the back of this form.*

- ❏ I want to help SRV's free Nectar distribution program ($50 and up)
- ❏ I want to help widen Nectar's distribution ($200 and up)
- ❏ I want to make sure there are future issues of Nectar ($500 and up)

Please fill out the back side of this form and mail it with your check to:
SRV Associations, PO Box 1364, Honokaa, HI 96727
MasterCard or Visa accepted ◆ Make checks payable to: SRV Associations
808-990-3354 ◆ srvinfo@srv.org ◆ www.srv.org   #28

Advaita-satya-amritam

NECTAR
of Non-Dual Truth

Donation/Order Form
Suggested donation $7 per issue

*Nectar is available for free if you write, email, or call for a copy.
Your generous donations make Nectar available to others and help us to widen our distribution.*

Those who donate $7 or more for the next issue, will be added to our subscriber's list.
- ❏ Please send me/my friend a free copy of the next issue of Nectar.
- ❏ Send me ___ copies to give to friends or a spiritual center of my choice.
- ❏ I am enclosing the names of persons/centers I want to receive Nectar. *Fill out the back of this form.*

- ❏ I want to help SRV's free Nectar distribution program ($50 and up)
- ❏ I want to help widen Nectar's distribution ($200 and up)
- ❏ I want to make sure there are future issues of Nectar ($500 and up)

Please fill out the back side of this form and mail it with your check to:
SRV Associations, PO Box 1364, Honokaa, HI 96727
MasterCard or Visa accepted ◆ Make checks payable to: SRV Associations
808-990-3354 ◆ srvinfo@srv.org ◆ www.srv.org   #28

Advaita-satya-amritam

NECTAR
of Non-Dual Truth

Donation/Order Form
Suggested donation $7 per issue

*Nectar is available for free if you write, email, or call for a copy.
Your generous donations make Nectar available to others and help us to widen our distribution.*

Those who donate $7 or more for the next issue, will be added to our subscriber's list.
- ❏ Please send me/my friend a free copy of the next issue of Nectar.
- ❏ Send me ___ copies to give to friends or a spiritual center of my choice.
- ❏ I am enclosing the names of persons/centers I want to receive Nectar. *Fill out the back of this form.*

- ❏ I want to help SRV's free Nectar distribution program ($50 and up)
- ❏ I want to help widen Nectar's distribution ($200 and up)
- ❏ I want to make sure there are future issues of Nectar ($500 and up)

Please fill out the back side of this form and mail it with your check to:
SRV Associations, PO Box 1364, Honokaa, HI 96727
MasterCard or Visa accepted ◆ Make checks payable to: SRV Associations
808-990-3354 ◆ srvinfo@srv.org ◆ www.srv.org   #28

Your Information:

Name: _____
Address: _____
City, State, Zip: _____
Email: _____

Additional Address: (please use a sheet of paper for more addresses)

Name: _____
Address: _____
City, State, Zip: _____
Email: _____

Do you wish to pay by Mastercard or Visa?
Card No.: _____ **Amount:** _____
Exp. date: _____ **Phone no.:** _____
Signature: _____

Questions? call SRV Associations: 808-990-3354

Your Information:

Name: _____
Address: _____
City, State, Zip: _____
Email: _____

Additional Address: (please use a sheet of paper for more addresses)

Name: _____
Address: _____
City, State, Zip: _____
Email: _____

Do you wish to pay by Mastercard or Visa?
Card No.: _____ **Amount:** _____
Exp. date: _____ **Phone no.:** _____
Signature: _____

Questions? call SRV Associations: 808-990-3354

Your Information:

Name: _____
Address: _____
City, State, Zip: _____
Email: _____

Additional Address: (please use a sheet of paper for more addresses)

Name: _____
Address: _____
City, State, Zip: _____
Email: _____

Do you wish to pay by Mastercard or Visa?
Card No.: _____ **Amount:** _____
Exp. date: _____ **Phone no.:** _____
Signature: _____

Questions? call SRV Associations: 808-990-3354